192 530 2950

S0-BZH-290

DeMille:
The Man and His Pictures

Other Books by Raymond Lee

Not So Dumb
Fit for the Chase
Faces of Hollywood (with Clarence Sinclair Bull)
Pearl White: the Peerless, Fearless Girl (with Manuel Weltman)
Gangsters and Hoodlums (with B. C. Van Hecke)
Gloria Swanson (with Richard M. Hudson)

By Gabe Essoe

Tarzan of the Movies
Films of Clark Gable

DeMille:

The Man and His Pictures

by
GABE ESSOE
and
RAYMOND LEE

SOUTH BRUNSWICK AND NEW YORK: A. S. BARNES AND COMPANY
LONDON: THOMAS YOSELOFF LTD

Library of Congress Catalogue Card Number: 79-88257

A. S. Barnes and Co., Inc.
Cranbury, New Jersey 08512

Thomas Yoseloff Ltd
108 New Bond Street
London W1Y OQX, England

ISBN 0-498-06909-5
Printed in the United States of America

for Marylee and Bill Beck

Contents

Acknowledgments

Great appreciation is expressed by the authors to all of those who helped make this book a reality, especially: Charlton Heston, Henry Wilcoxon, Elmer Bernstein, Art Arthur, Charles Bickford, Paul S. Eriksson, George Thomas, Magdalene Maskell, Loraine Burdick, Gabriella Essoe; Donna Hyatt for proofreading; the library staff of the Academy of Motion Picture Arts and Sciences; Mike Berman, Paramount Pictures Corporation; John Lebold, Gunnard Nelson, B. C. Van Hecke; MGM Studios; Fred H. Wright, Mike Santoro, Myron Braum, Sam O'Campos for photographs.

DeMille:
The Man and His Pictures

*DeMille's Bible**

In my 43 years in Hollywood I have passed many milestones marking the progress of our industry.

None has ever loomed larger in my mind—or moved me to deeper appreciation—than this Milestone Award of the Screen Producers' Guild, coming as it does from my fellow-craftsmen, the men of my own profession, who know our work from the inside and from top to bottom, and who have thought me worthy to receive this award, one of the highest and most coveted of Hollywood's honors.

I am deeply grateful.

No one knows better than you that motion pictures are an industry, and an art, in which no one stands alone. The debate will go on for a long time over whether the producer or the director, the writer, the cameraman or the editor or the actor is the most important and responsible artist in the production of a motion picture. We need not try to settle that debate tonight. The fact that the question is debated is proof that we are greatly dependent upon each.

So, when you honor one individual, you are honoring all who have worked with him, and all from whose work he has learned and benefited. In my case their names would make a very lengthy list.

It is a deeply moving experience to see so many of them here tonight—especially to stand in the reflected glory of so many stars who have lent their brilliance to DeMille pictures, from the first *Squaw Man* to the second *Ten Commandments,* and who tonight have filled my heart by this wonderful tribute.

And I am particularly happy that sitting with me at this table are the two young men I used to join at a much more modest table 43 years ago—two young men who have carved their names on imperishable milestones along the path of motion picture history. Without them I would not be here—my first partners: Jesse Lasky and Samuel Goldwyn.

* (Mr. DeMille gave this address upon receiving the Milestone Award of the Screen Producers' Guild at a dinner in the Beverly Hilton Hotel on January 22, 1956).

I cannot name all whose presence here multiplies my happiness this evening—for I would have to name everyone in the room.

But I cannot stand here, surrounded by so many friends old and young, including some who were not born when I first came to Hollywood, without thinking of others who did so much to make our industry great and who are now gone out of this world of shadows and images into the Light.

I cannot think of them and of their work, without wishing again, as I have wished many times, that we and the public were more aware of the dramatic riches we have stored in our vaults—the classics of the screen.

Of course we have occasional reissues, if one must use that detestable word. We do not say that someone reissues *Hamlet* or *Lohengrin,* or that the next time you go to the Louvre you can see a reissue of the Mona Lisa. You might as well say that God reissues the sunset every evening.

When we think in terms of "reissues" we automatically condemn the picture to second-rate treatment by the publicity and advertising departments, by the exhibitors, and by the public.

The great classics of the screen deserve better treatment. They are not second-rate, but first-rate, specimens of the motion picture art.

And I include among them a number of silent pictures, which, for pure motion picture art, have not been surpassed by sound. These should be presented to the public on special projecting machines running at 60 feet a minute instead of the present 90 feet a minute that makes great artists jump about like Woody Woodpecker.

This industry will not come of age until it makes a determined effort to keep its own great classics alive by presenting them regularly to the public in a manner worthy of their merit and worthy of the great names of those who made them.

Among that host of names there is one that towers like a mountain. His spirit and influence are present in every gathering of motion picture people. His hand can be seen in every film that is made—David Wark Griffith.

Many years ago, some people used to flatter me by saying that Griffith and I were rivals. Griffith had no rivals. He was the teacher of us all.

Motion picture historians are saying now—and truly enough—that Griffith did not invent the close-up or cross-cutting or some of the other techniques with which he has been credited. But this does not take away from his glory. He did something more important than to invent those techniques. He was the first to realize fully their dramatic value; the first to raise them to the level of a fine art; the first to give the motion picture camera its own unique and fluent language. Griffith was the first to photograph thought.

We all learned that from him—and we have been using it ever since. But if we are the heirs of Griffith, and of the other pioneers, we have inherited also a great responsibility. We should be humble when we hear learned students of the arts maintain that motion pictures are, or can be, the highest and most popular form of art the world has ever known. Only music approaches motion pictures in universal appeal—and not even music has the impact of our pictures.

Mr. Frank Freeman, head of Paramount Studios, has told us the astonishing figures of world attendance at DeMille pictures. The figures are staggering—but the imagination falters when we try to assess the influence our pictures have upon the billions who see them. Your mail undoubtedly brings you the same testimony that mine brings me.

Here is part of a letter I received while I was in Egypt, from the Prime Minister of Pakistan, concerning *The Ten Commandments:*

> I . . . hope that your latest effort in promoting a better understanding of the ideologies of the three greatest living religions of this world will succeed.
>
> At a time when all our moral and religious values are in jeopardy from a new atheistic pseudo-religious creed, it is imperative that there should be a greater understanding, fuller cooperation and much goodwill between the peoples of these three great religions, so that a combined and coordinated effort may be made to safeguard our respective Cultures and Traditions.
>
> God has given you a most powerful medium for the projection of thoughts and ideas and I sincerely hope that you will undertake with missionary zeal the task of producing films which will have this definite objective in view . . . so as to safeguard our free and democratic way of life.

Unquote from Mohammed Ali.

When leaders of nations tell us—as the highest officials of Egypt and Burma have told me—that as boys they derived their conception of the world, their ideas of right and wrong, from American motion pictures, they bring home to us our awe-inspiring responsibility. It is a sobering thought that the decisions we make at our desks in Hollywood may intimately affect the lives of men, women, and children throughout the world.

As I see it, our responsibility is twofold. We are responsible as artists, and as molders of men's thoughts. We have a duty to our art, and a duty to our audience. These two responsibilities must be kept clearly in view at all times.

If we do so, we may be able to keep our industry free of the forces which threaten to corrupt it from within, and those which threaten to cramp and stifle it from without.

Our greatest danger from within the industry is the worship of the golden calf—the temptation to care nothing about what we produce as long as it makes money. Of course, any business must make a profit. Sir Henry Irving, one of the greatest artists of the stage, said the theatre "must be carried on as a business or it will fail as an art." But we betray our responsibilities, if money-making is the only goal we seek in our business.

Perhaps we think that vice sells at a higher price than virtue. Unfortunately, it often does in this world. It is *easier* to draw a crowd by pandering to its lowest tastes than by inspiring its highest ideals. But is it treason to the human spirit—and treason to the art we serve? And we are simply stupid if we have not learned that, in motion pictures, dirt is not necessarily pay dirt.

Take four of the biggest grossing pictures ever made—*Gone With the Wind, Going My Way, The Robe,* and *The Greatest Show on Earth.* Any one of them is a picture you could take your children to without having to brainwash them afterwards.

There is another way also that the golden calf rears his head in our industry—the tendency of some of us to pull apart, instead of pulling together, the tendency of some groups within the industry to grab all they can for themselves without regard for the industry as a whole. This industry will not survive if management tries to run it without regard for labor, or if labor tries to wreck its economic structure by unrealistic and unreasonable demands, or if agents misuse the power which their control of talent gives them, or if exhibitors forget they are showmen and that good exhibition demands as much showmanship as good production does.

Yet at the same time I need hardly tell this audience that it is not the primary business of motion pictures to preach sermons, or to distort the truth by showing a picture of the world which leaves out the fact that life has a seamy side.

There are well-meaning people who want art to be so antiseptic that, if they had their way, art would no longer be a mirror held up to nature. These good people try very hard to get their way—sometimes by censorship, sometimes through organized and disciplined pressure groups.

I stress the fact that these people mean well but they know not what they do. We are in agreement with them in that neither motion pictures, nor any other art, has the right to corrupt morals. But motion pictures should be judged as an art—by judges who know what they are talking about.

There is one Biblical subject I have long wanted to produce. I have done considerable work on it, at considerable expense. But I was halted when one influential religious leader, after reading my treatment of the subject said, and I quote him: "You simply cannot show anything evil in the same picture with the spotless purity of this subject."

This kind of thinking betrays a lack of understanding.

A motion picture requires drama and action. Drama means conflict. You cannot show the brightness of good unless you show it in contrast to the darkness of evil. Nor can you do it by putting preachments in the mouths of your characters.

Some professional moralists tell us that art should ennoble and strengthen character. Strong characters are not formed by being blindfolded and wrapped in cotton wool.

Life is a warfare between good and evil—and, as the great Puritan poet, John Milton, put it, "He that can apprehend and consider vice with all her baits and seeming pleasures, and yet abstain, and yet distinguish, and yet prefer that which is truly better, he is the true warfaring Christian."

The really great moralists—men who have thought deeply on the problem of art and morals—have understood that.

Only a few months ago, the Catholic Bishops of Germany observed that "to call things by their right names, and to recognize the power of evil in the world, is of great value" precisely because it "gives rise to shocks which can have a wholesome effect." They expressed their gratitude to writers who "mirror reality" as it is, instead of painting a "sentimentalized . . . untrue picture" of human existence, its struggles, defeats, and triumphs."

This broad and deep understanding of the function of art is a far cry from the pettiness of censors whose whole idea of morality is apparently bound by the length of a skirt and the depth of a bodice.

It would truly be immoral for us to portray a world that contained no evil, or a world in which evil was never strong or alluring. It would be immoral because it would be untrue. We would really be corrupting the minds of youth if we taught them that they are living in a world where virtue triumphs uncontested. What is more corrupting than to be taught a lie?

In a very real sense we are defending morality when we fight censorship, and when we refuse to yield to the ridiculous demands of pressure groups. I am not saying all their demands are ridiculous. But some of the demands, in your experience and mine, certainly are.

Censorship is not the answer—but neither is unbridled license. Our responsibility as artists, and as molders of thought, makes great demands upon us—and the greatest is the demand for self-discipline.

We do well to fight censorship—but we must do it by giving it no legitimate grounds for attacking us, while defending to the full our right to portray the world as it is. You may say that I am asking the motion picture industry to walk along a razor's edge with deep pitfalls on either side. And perhaps I am. I have never said or thought that being molders of the world's thought was an easy job. But that is one reason why, after 43 years, I still find it the most challenging, the greatest job on earth.

Motion pictures have been my life's work. And every foot of it in film, and every minute of it in time, has been an adventure which I would not exchange for anything else in the world.

We in the industry hold great power. Who else—except the missionaries of God—has had our opportunity to make the brotherhood of man not a phrase, but a reality—a brotherhood that has shared the same laughter and the same tears, dreamt the same dreams, been encouraged by the same hopes, inspired by the same faith in man and in God, which we painted for them, night after night, on the screens of the world? Our influence must be used for good—for truth, for beauty, and for freedom.

Let us remember Winston Churchill's words: "Those who serve supreme causes do not consider what they can get, but what they can give. Let that be our privilege . . . in the years that lie before us."

1

"We have rented a barn in Hollywood...."

A grey noonday in 1912: two young New York theatrical producers were lunching at the Claridge Grill comparing notes on their latest failures—a play, *Cheer Up,* and a musical patterned after the *Folies Bergère.*

"Cecil, why don't we try our luck in another field?"

"Well, Jesse, I was seriously thinking of joining a revolution—any revolution!"

"How about motion pictures? My brother-in-law, Sam Goldfish, and his lawyer-friend, Arthur Friend, believe it's the new entertainment medium. All we need is $20,000. I can put up five, and I know Sam and Arthur have their share. Surely you can raise five!"

"I've lost my shirt in *Cheer Up.* But it sounds more exciting than a revolution. Maybe I can borrow my share from my brother William. Every play he's written has been a hit. I'll talk to him!"

An arm-waving Sam Goldfish rushed to their table, almost knocking the tray from the hands of the delivering waiter.

"I'm ruined! I'm ruined! I knew that new Democratic Congress would wreck the country!"

Jesse and Cecil dipped into their soup.

"Fellows, don't you understand?" continued Sam, pulling up a chair. "Congress just lifted the duty on gloves. The bottom's dropped out of my market. I've just been put outa business. Gotta get into something new."

Jesse's eyes stared like an owl's behind his glasses. He said, "Sam, what about that idea you and Arthur Friend have been talking about so much—making movies?"

The Lasky Co. Standing (l. to r.): Oscar Apfel, Alex Figman, Charles Richman, Wilfred Buckland, Theodore Roberts, Robert Edeson, Edward Abeles, Cecil B. DeMille. Seated (l. to r.): Lolita Robertson, Jesse L. Lasky, Bessie Barriscale.

"Why not? I mean, what's there to lose. I have lost it all." He turned to the waiter, who had just approached, and said, "I'll have whatever they're having."

Jesse and Cecil eyebrowed each other and then forked their salads.

"OK, Jesse. But we'll need a fourth partner."

"Not if you count me in," Cecil said.

As Sam and Cecil shook hands, Jesse turned over the menu, and, writing in pencil, outlined the terms of a contract forming the Jesse L. Lasky Feature Play Company with Cecil B. DeMille, who had never seen a movie, as director-general, Sam Goldfish as salesman, Arthur Friend as legal aid and Lasky as the titular head.

Later, Cecil excitedly repeated the goings-on at the Grill to his brother William, who gave him some fraternal advice: "Sorry, C. Can't do it. The project doesn't sound like it will hold water. But I will guarantee your return to New York when you get stranded in the wild, wild west!"

But Cecil nevertheless was convinced that the new partners stood a fair chance of making a go of it. He hocked everything he owned

DeMille directing first Squaw Man, *1914.*

The Squaw Man *company waits C.B.'s order to work, 1914.*

and raised a little over $3,000 with which he became the fourth partner.

For their first subject, Lasky and DeMille selected the 1905 stage hit *The Squaw Man,* by Edwin Milton Royle.

The plot went like this: An Englishman covers up a friend's embezzlement by shipping out to Wyoming. An Indian maid saves his life in a gun fight. They marry and she bears him a child. Back in England his fiancee proves his innocence and comes west. The Indian maid kills herself and the Englishman and his fiancee return with his son to their home.

They selected *The Squaw Man* (1913) more for economic than artistic reasons. Being a western, most of the scenes would be shot outdoor, which would cut down production costs. They decided Arizona was the best location.

William Faversham had created the role on Broadway and Dustin Farnum had toured the country with it. Faversham was not available; Farnum was. They offered him an interest in lieu of salary but he balked and demanded $250 a week and a four-week guarantee. He got it.

The cast credits of The Squaw Man *marked the first time this information was ever presented in a moving picture.*

In this scene from The Squaw Man, *Dustin Farnum (center) listens to Dick Lareno's tale. DeMille (on the far right) played a gambler because the company didn't have enough money to hire extras.*

With their star secure, the Jesse L. Lasky Feature Play Company set out by train for high adventure in America's last pioneer land. En route DeMille and Oscar Apfel, who had some previous film directing experience, began adapting the play for the screen. Several days later, light-headed with the drama and action, they climbed off the train at Flagstaff.

Quickly surveying the landscape, C.B. summoned cameraman Alfred Gandolfi. Arizona was beautiful, healthy and sunny, but Arizona was not Wyoming, where Gandolfi had hunted. Arizona was all wrong for the story. The puffing of the steam engine accented their dilemma. The train whistle screamed and the conductor shouted "All aboard!" The Jesse L. Lasky Feature Play Company, decidedly disappointed in the Arizona scenery, made their first artistic decision.

The director-general shouted the official order.

"Re-board!"

Legs and arms and luggage scrambled as the train lurched forward and the men leaped on and out of Flagstaff. In the swaying Club car the director-general counted heads and issued his second order.

"No one leaves this train until the end of the line—Los Angeles, California." And then he turned to Oscar, "I hear you can make pictures there against any kind of background and the sun shines almost all the time!"

Several days later the New York office of the Jesse L. Lasky Feature Play Company, established in the Longacre Theatre Building, was shocked with the following telegram from DeMille:

"We have rented a barn in Hollywood for two hundred dollars a month . . ."

On December 29, 1913, a special sun spotlighted the barn of Jacob Stern at the corner of Selma and Vine Streets in Hollywood, a few miles west of Los Angeles.

The Lasky Company actors took their places in an exterior set built on a raised wooden platform. The director-general shouted: "Action! Camera!" The making of movieland's first full-length feature had begun—a western to boot.

For DeMille's office a partition was set up within the barn to form a small room. A desk was brought in for him and a kitchen table for his as yet nonexistent secretary. And they were ready for business. The most important article of furniture, according to the director-general, was the wastebasket. "It provided a very convenient refuge for my feet whenever Mr. Stern washed his carriage and the water ran under my desk."

But there was little refuge from the Trust, the Motion Picture Patents Company, which had been organized by Thomas A. Edison to protect the movies that he invented in 1889. It enabled him to force a monopoly over motion picture production in America. Producers were faced with joining the Trust or quitting business. If a producer refused to go along with the Trust, they found cameras impossible to buy; theatres became unwilling to show their films; a mysterious run of accidents would suddenly plague their studio; rolls of film would catch fire; and occasionally shooting sessions would become fist-swinging riots.

The Trust's grip on film production was broken only through the unrelenting efforts and independent spirit of such aggressive film makers as DeMille, William Fox and Carl Laemmle.

To emphasize their intentions, Trust agents broke into the Lasky Laboratory and destroyed the first week's shooting on *Squaw Man*. But DeMille, realizing that film was a flammable product, wisely had two negatives printed of every scene. The first in the business to take this precaution, he stored one at home and one at the

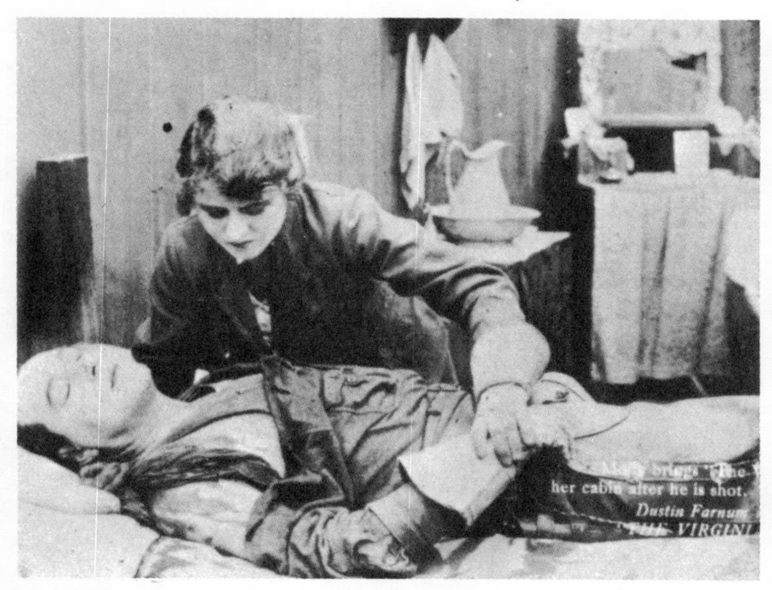

Winifred Kingston and Dustin Farnum in The Virginian, *1914.*

Theodore Roberts, House Peters in The Girl of the Golden West.

Producer-partners Jesse Lasky, Adolph Zukor, Sam Goldwyn, and Albert Kaufman, 1915.

laboratory. So he won the first round against the Trust without stepping into the ring.

Shortly thereafter, anonymous letters with words clipped from newspapers and pasted together began arriving at the office threatening his life if he didn't get out of the movie business. Refusing to be intimidated, C. B. purchased a revolver and kept it tucked in his belt. He wore it on the set to let the Trust know that he meant to resist them.

He also slept in the laboratory from time to time to protect his valuable films. And because it was a short, pleasant distance from his home on Cahuenga Boulevard to the studio-barn, he bought a horse for transportation. The exercise kept him trim.

He once remarked to his star, Farnum, "With my revolver and horse, I should be in the picture with you, rather than directing it."

One evening while riding home, a shot from a clump of trees almost cracked his eardrum. C. B. reined his horse and drew his gun, but he could hear only the evening breeze rustling the eucalpti.

DeMille continued to listen intently for a few moments, but hearing nothing, he proceeded homeward.

"Someone tried again, in the same place and same way, a few days later," C. B. recalled years later. "But this time from a greater distance and with no better luck. I have never tried to shoot anybody, but if ever I get tired of merely shooting pictures and decide to take up a little assassination on the side, I hope I shall be more business-like than that unknown gunman of Cahuenga Pass. He must have felt terribly frustrated for, after his two futile attempts, he gave up. I wonder if he is in that photograph on the wall of my office I took that first day of the whole company. Well, he deserves to be. He was the first critic of a DeMille picture."

Although the Trust had apparently decided to let the new company continue, lack of funds threatened a halt to activities. Riding home from a location in San Fernando Valley with Eugene de Rue, father of Carmen, who played the Indian Boy Hal in *Squaw Man,* C. B. approached him about buying an interest in the company.

De Rue believed in the potential of motion pictures and assured him he would do everything to raise some money. When he was unsuccessful, C. B. informed him that a man by the name of W. W. Hodkinson had come up with a sizeable sum. Years later Hodkinson sold his interest in the resultant giant Paramount Studios for $5 million.

When one realizes the millions DeMille later spent on his spectacles at which supposedly wiser heads shook, and supposedly more konwledgeable voices clucked, "This time he's gone too far"—and later were amazed at his enormous profits, a little item of three dollars is quite a curio in his career.

A scene in *Squaw Man* called for a faro dealer at the cost of three dollars. When DeMille consulted the budget and found out that after paying the whole company he wouldn't have three dollars, he played the part himself.

Finally Hollywood's first feature was finished and Jesse Lasky traveled out from New York hosting VIPs entrained for the gala screening.

But the real drama of that evening was not on the screen. It was in the audience which had gathered with such high hopes. The lights in the makeshift project room dimmed. The title of *The Squaw Man* went on the screen—and promptly skittered off at the top of the screen. The actors appeared, and as promptly climbed out of sight, sometimes leaving their feet at the top of the screen

DeMille inspects Monte Blue's makeup for The Captive, *1915.*

Ina Claire, Tom Forman, Theodore Roberts, and Helen Marlborough in The Wild Goose Chase.

and their heads peeking up from the bottom. The effect was the same as is seen on television when the vertical tuner is not properly adjusted.

"*The Squaw Man* was running away from us," C. B. wrote later. "We tried again, with the same effect. There was nothing to do but turn up the house lights and send the gaily gathered audience home, amid the kind of subdued, inconsequential, well-meant murmurs that one might hear from the guests if death suddenly struck at a dinner party."

Sabotage was the first thought. But all the equipment checked out. What had happened? It just didn't figure.

But Sam Goldfish, who later changed his name to Sam Goldwyn and became a producer who didn't have to stand in anyone's shadow, came up with an idea.

"Bring the negative," he said. "Pop Lubin can save us if anybody can." Sigmund "Pop" Lubin was one of the original seven members of the Trust, a pioneer film maker who knew all there was to know about moving pictures.

DeMille, Sam and Lasky sped to New York with the print in tin boxes and C. B. carried his trusty revolver in his belt which upset Jesse no end. After all New York was not the wild west. DeMille argued, "Just in case."

In Lubin's office they waited. Fifteen minutes seemed like hours. They felt they were waiting for the coroner's report. Lubin was a member of the Trust. Why had they trusted him? Sam said Lubin had given his word.

Pop smiled as he returned.

"Gentlemen, relax. There is nothing wrong with your film. We'll fix it."

All that had been wrong was the director-general's Dutch thrift. During the 18 days of *The Squaw Man's* production, he had come across a bargain: a secondhand, British-made machine for punching the sprocket holes along the side of the negative film. The man who sold it to C. B. may have pointed out that his machine punched 65 sprocket holes per foot of film. "If he did," C. B. reasoned, "I am sure I nodded wisely. What I had no notion of was the fact that all our other equipment and positive film were sprocketed at 64 holes to the foot." The difference between 1/64th and 1/65th of a foot was enough to account for the erratic behavior of the picture. The solution was simplicity itself. It was one of those things anyone could have figured out—anyone, that is, who knew motion picture photog-

Edgar Selwyn as The Arab, *1915.*

raphy as Lubin knew it. Lubin's technicians simply pasted a thin strip of film over the edge of the negative, perforated it properly at 64, and the Jesse L. Lasky Feature Play Company was back in business.

Why did Pop Lubin help? Maybe the American dream was reflected in the eyes of his young competitors, and he knew no one could strangle freedom of expression for long.

The ultimate triumph of *The Squaw Man* was described by brother Bill, the doubter:

"As I sat in that dark auditorium and felt the ebb and flow of the play, just as if it were being played in the flesh before me, and felt, too, how it was holding the whole audience until they were under the spell as much as they could have been in the living theatre, I had my first vision of what this new art was bound to become; how it was, inevitably, to serve untold millions of people.

"In spite of its obvious faults, limitations and silences, I saw unrolled before my eyes the first really new form of dramatic storytelling which had been invented in some five hundred years . . ."

Significantly, *The Squaw Man* represented a great many innovations in the infant medium of moving pictures. It was the longest film to have been made to that time, six reels. No Broadway play had ever been filmed before. With no experience, DeMille made the picture for $15,000, an investment which was going to return a quarter of a million dollars, maturing the infant company overnight.

Prior to this time, moving picture players were unknown to audiences, Mary Pickford, for example, was a nameless star, familiar to thousands before she was identified on the screen. Borrowing on his stage experience, DeMille figured that an audience should have a program and created screen credits to introduce his cast of characters in *Squaw Man.* It was a practice which was immediately picked up by other film makers.

In those early days very few indoor scenes were made because of the difficulty in lighting. Sunlight was admitted through an open roof and sides of the studio, and scenes were taken against a single-wall background. On rainy days, all work ceased. Indoor lighting was used for the first time when DeMille fixed up a couple of spotlights on a foggy day, again borrowing from his theatre background.

With *Squaw Man,* Hollywood became the film center in the world and remained so until the death of DeMille.

Although Oscar Apfel shared both producing and directorial credits with C. B. on *Squaw Man,* from that point on DeMille produced and directed all his later films.

C. B., on April 14, 1914, began his initial solo direction of the best-selling novel and stage hit, *The Virginian,* and C. B.'s "accident film" was born. Here DeMille started his sometimes humorous, some-

Thomas Meighan and Charlotte Walker in Kindling, *1915.*

times tragic, collection of accidents on the set.

One scene as scripted showed leading lady Winifred Kingston and villain Monroe Salisbury seated on the ground talking. Dustin Farnum angrily rides up and shoots straight at Salisbury. But when the camera focuses on Salisbury's feet, the audience gets a double jolt—a dead rattler is sprawled out and not Salisbury.

DeMille had imported two magnificent Texas rattlers for the scene through the Los Angeles Zoo, which was to receive the remaining snake. The first take went beautifully with Farnum riding up and shooting at the camera which then cut to Salisbury's legs and the dead rattler. And a surprise. Somehow the spare rattler had escaped his confinement and slithered in between Salisbury's legs beside the other snake and coiled to strike.

DeMille quickly assured his noted actor that there was nothing to worry about because the critter had been defanged, but glancing to the white-faced prop man for reassurance, he numbed.

"He ain't defanged, Mr. DeMille. The zoo didn't and I didn't!"

DeMille directing Max Figman and Lolita Robinson in What's His Name? *(1914).*

The DeMille voice, which would later thunder thousands of movie extras into action, turned as pianissimo as a mouse as he advised Salisbury not to move—not one move—not even to breathe. Slowly the snake unwound and sidled toward a clump of sage brush. In that instant, Frank Hopkins, a cowboy C. B. had hired for such an emergency, shot the rattler's head off. And with the camera having recorded the entire incident, DeMille began his "accident film."

Following the critical and financial success of *The Virginian,* DeMille from late 1914 to mid 1915 created a solid foundation for his later cinema work with: *The Call of the North, What's His Name?, The Man from Home, Rose of the Rancho, Girl of the Golden West, The Warrens of Virginia, The Unafraid, The Captive, Wild Goose Chase, The Arab, Chimmie Fadden,* and *Kindling.*

Of the ten pictures after *The Squaw Man,* Oscar Apfel directed eight and DeMille two. Apfel ground them out like sausages, one every three or four weeks. DeMille was much more painstaking, and as his flair for sweeping dramatic spectacle developed, his shooting schedules expanded from five to six to seven and then eight weeks.

In his deliberation, he became responsible for many innovations in the interest of pictorial realism and would stop at nothing to give his pictures "class." This passion got to be a severe strain on the budget in later years, but in 1914 he managed it for the price of a black velvet backdrop. His brother's play, *The Warrens of Virginia,* became the first picture to show interior night scenes without blazing sunlight streaming into all the doors and windows.

By manipulating sunlight reflectors, he became the first director to vary light intensity in scenes where stage directions called for someone to turn down a lamp or knock it over in a struggle. Then he went further in his experiments with light and shade, striving for artistic composition and pattern. Up to this time, sharpness of detail was the sole criterion by which motion picture photography was judged. A scene was highly praised if you could see all the wrinkles in a man's pants.

DeMille rejected this standard as false and in *The Unafraid* he achieved some startling and thrilling shadowy effects by backlighting and sidelighting his actors. But when the film reached New York for distribution, Sam Goldfish exploded in protest, demanding to know how the hell they expected him to sell a picture in which the lighting was "so lousy that you can't even see the characters' faces half the time."

Upon getting Goldfish's reaction, Lasky wired DeMille for advice.

This picture, which was sent out by the A.P. wirephoto at the time of Demille's death at 77, shows him as he had looked 44 years before, working in his office. Behind him is a poster advertising his first motion picture. Note the famous puttees.

C. B. shrugged impatiently and wired back that Sam must be blind. Couldn't he see that they were the first to use a new artistic technique, a breakthrough that they should all be proud of.

Goldfish somehow found it hard to be proud of a film where the actors were often obscured by darkness. But armed with the assurance that the murky shadows were art and not carelessness, he hiked the rental fees for the picture and made a killing.

This incident and many like it created an early aura around DeMille. It was in this pioneering period that his brother William succumbed to the Hollywood lure and joined C. B. as writer and, later, as director.

As exhilarating as this era of growth was to DeMille, it was laced with tragedy. An ill-fated scene in *The Captive,* a Blanche Sweet vehicle, added the most cruel episode to C. B.'s "accident film."

The action called for a group of soldiers to fire into a door and then break it down. "Now boys," directed C. B., "I've had that door made strong, so it will take some real breaking into. We'll only do it once, and there won't be any fake about it. So go after it hard!"

With wild yells the little band rushed at the door and started to batter it down. As the first steel-shod butts crashed against the wood a volley of shots rang out, and one of the regular cowboys—big, good-natured Bob Fleming, who was in the second rank—quietly sank to the ground and died, shot through the head.

Somehow, one rifle had been loaded with a live cartridge. Although all the guns were supposed to be loaded with blanks, the careless extra who wielded that rifle had not checked his weapon out thoroughly before going into action. The property boys all swore that they had examined every piece before handing them out.

It was a sad group that abandoned the studio early that afternoon. But the show had to go on and the scene was made the following day. "Nerve-racking, of course," William DeMille recalled later, "but that's pictures."

The widow of the man who was killed was kept on the studio payroll for many years. DeMille once wondered "if her suffering was any greater than that of the man who carried with him to his own grave the memory of having taken another's life so uselessly?"

Since many guns had been going off simultaneously, it was never determined who was responsible. But one man never returned to the set after that day. DeMille knew that no one could really be held completely accountable, and wisely played down the accident as much as possible.

As the Lord of Film's first "day" ended, with the gloom of death still lingering in the twilight hours, an earth-shaking challenge was lying in wait for the second. Jesse L. Lasky informed C. B. that he had signed the world famous opera star, Geraldine Farrar, to a contract and had assigned DeMille to direct the volcanic beauty in recreating one of her greatest roles, *Carmen.*

"Carmen?" sighed C. B., "Without using her glorious voice?"

2

An extrasensory perception made him aware ...

As the train pulled into the Santa Fe station in Los Angeles, a band struck up strains from *Carmen* and a host of teenage "Gerry-Flappers" screamed adoration for their arriving idol.

Jesse Lasky, his honor Mayor Henry R. Rose, and other city dignitaries waited as the door to her private car was opened and the world's reigning opera diva, Geraldine Farrar, stepped down, followed by her parents, personal manager Morris Gest and his wife, and a bevy of press agents.

Presented with a bouquet of American Beauty roses, La Farrar and party walked down a red carpet that stretched from the platform through the depot and to a waiting limousine.

Lasky and Goldfish, who at this time changed his name to Goldwyn, saw to it that Farrar was given the full treatment. Her contract commanded $300 a week, the largest salary the company ever paid an actress. A private railway car was also always at her disposal. A two-story mansion with butler, cook, and maid and a limousine with chauffeur provided all the comforts she could want. At the studio, a specially built bungalow with a grand piano provided for her the proper atmosphere in which to prepare for her role.

After welcoming Miss Farrar, C. B. began mulling over her first appearance before a motion picture camera. He fully appreciated her talents as opera's finest, but how well would she come across in a medium so foreign to her own? Moving pictures were something entirely different, and nothing in her background could give her the posture required for films other than film experience itself. To make a costly production like *Carmen* (1915) on a trial basis seemed foolhardy.

DeMille directing Geraldine Farrar and Wallace Reid in Carmen, *1915.*

DeMille decided that they should make another picture first and allow Miss Farrar to grow accustomed to the picture business. "If we make *Carmen* first," he reasoned with Lasky, "then we will probably have to junk a lot of it. We've got another property, *Maria Rosa,* a Spanish love story that is much like *Carmen.* Let's let her cut her moving picture teeth on that and then make *Carmen.* I'll warrant that she'll give a good second performance. Then we can hold up the release of *Maria Rosa* until after the public's seen her in *Carmen.*"

Lasky saw the merit in C. B.'s argument. And Miss Farrar, who'd been apprehensive of mastering the different acting techniques required for the movies, was quick to agree.

Set at ease by this production of lesser importance, Miss Farrar progressed beautifully. Her poise before the lens came as no surprise to DeMille. He expected it.

Geraldine Farrar's co-star in *Maria Rosa* was an unknown, Wallace Reid, whom DeMille had liked and took a chance on. The young former stage actor was so good that C. B. gave him the tragic role of Don Jose in *Carmen.*

"I have not always been right in my estimation of players," the lord of film commented years later. "Whenever I see the tremendous

Gypsies Wallace Reid and Geraldine Farrar in Maria Rosa, *1915.*

Stars (l. to r.) Ernest Joy, Pedro de Cordoba, Geraldine Farrar, and Wallace Reid in Maria Rosa.

Geraldine Farrar as Carmen, *1915.*

magnetism of Clark Gable on the screen and think of his unchallenged and enduring popularity, I shrink a little inside myself, remembering that I once declared pontifically that he did not have what it takes for a successful career in films. And Clark Gable is not the only one about whom I have been wrong. But I was right about Wallace Reid."

Because *Maria Rosa* was withheld from release according to C.B.'s plan, the public saw Reid first as a star in *Carmen*. From then on, his rise was steady, until the terrible circumstances surrounding his death shattered his following. The shock of his passing multiplied explosively when it became known that he died at age thirty of drug addiction.

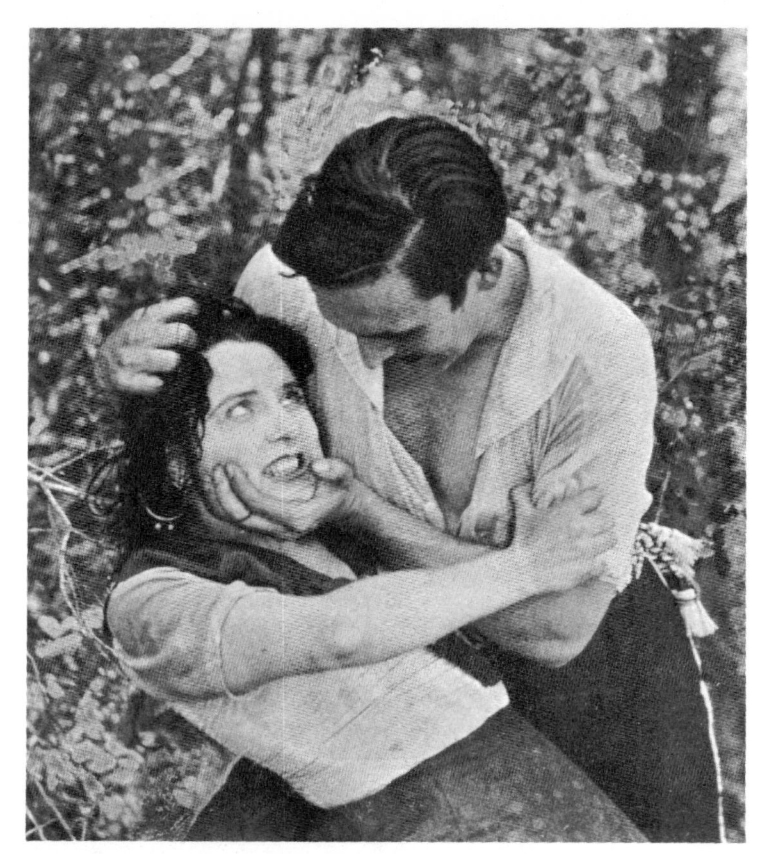

Wallace Reid and Geraldine Farrar engaged in a quarrel (Carmen).

DeMille, who had known about Reid's addiction long before his death, stood firm in his appraisal. He insisted that the public never realized the heroic efforts Reid had made to break his need for drugs. "The public is too quick to judge," C. B. protested. "I prefer to remember the brave determination in what Wally said to me just before he entered the sanitorium where he died: "I'll either come out cured, or I won't come out.' "

Carmen was a milestone in DeMille's career too. It earned him the title of "Hollywood's most contrasty director." Cameraman Alvin Wyckoff liked bright lights, but C. B. said that there were shadows in nature and that the mingling of darkness and light was more beautiful than flat glare. As with most things, C. B. won and he never lost the tag of being "contrasty" either.

An expression of love between Victor Moore and Mrs. Lewis McCord (Chimmie Fadden Out West, *1915*) .

A mysterious encounter for Fanny Ward and Sessue Hayakawa in The Cheat, *1915.*

The Trail of the Lonesome Pine *(1916) was taken from a play by Eugene Walter and John Fox, Jr. and adapted by DeMille. Charlotte Walker and Earle Fox are pictured.*

Elliott Dexter comforts Marie Doro in The Heart of Nora Flynn *(1916).*

DeMille in conference with Adolph Zukor and Jeanie MacPherson.

And thanks to brother Bill, the company didn't have to pay royalty to George Bizet for use of his libretto in making the film. Bizet had come forward and demanded an enormous sum of money for his property. Had they paid, C. B. would have had to sacrifice the quality of detail that he prided himself on.

But Bill DeMille had an answer. He figured that Carmen was Carmen whether it was Bizet or Prosper Merimee. After all Bizet had borrowed from Merimee's novel. Why couldn't they? All they had done was to cut out the middle man. No royalties had to be paid.

As C. B. could have predicted, *Carmen* was a first in many respects. Among other things, this film introduced the first fight between two women to the silent screen. Slight but spunky Jeanie MacPherson was chosen to play the cigarette girl who brawls with Carmen.

They rehearsed the bout for nearly a day, but the minute they began to shoot, the rehearsal was forgotten and the girls appeared to be fighting for real. And not willing to be outdone by the other, each continued in earnest. The results were spectacular.

And C. B., who could recognize a good performance in the dark, kept the camera rolling.

Simultaneous with C. B.'s production, another version of *Carmen* was being filmed. William Fox had learned of DeMille's film and decided to launch a quickie and beat him to the punch. In the title role, Fox cast Theda Bara, the original screen vamp, whom he had created two years earlier.

Geraldine Farrar on horseback in the title role of Joan the Woman, *1917. This was DeMille's first "mob scene."*

Reverent Joan of Arc, Geraldine Farrar.

Wallace Reid in Joan the Woman.

Wallace Reid and Geraldine Farrar in Joan the Woman.

Due to difficulties suffered by Fox's company, both films were released at the same time. Farrar's interpretation greatly outshone Bara's and the Fox copy-catter was withdrawn in embarrassment.

Following *Carmen,* the supply of available works suitable for moving pictures dwindled and their prices mounted. In an effort to broaden the supply, C. B. dangled an experimental offer of $250 for original stories before his writers, who had heretofore only adapted material from other sources.

Jeanie MacPherson, who had abandoned acting for a writing career, rose to the bait and delivered a splendid manuscript called *The Golden Chance* (1916). Another work, *The Cheat* (1916), turned in by Hector Turnbull, also qualified for the bonus.

C. B., who saw *The Golden Chance* as a perfect vehicle for Wally Reid and was intrigued by the plot of *The Cheat,* undertook the task of directing both at the same time because the company was in need of product.

The Cheat concerned a society woman who gambles away Red Cross funds and is forced to borrow $10,000 from a wealthy Japanese

Young Ben Alexander and handsome Raymond Hatton are two of Mary Pickford's admirers in The Little American.

Mary Pickford and Jack Holt in The Little American.

admirer with the promise that she will become his mistress. When she tries to repay him in cash, he brands her on the shoulder with the same mark he uses to identify all his possessions. After her enraged husband shoots him, she saves him from imprisonment by baring her branded shoulder in open court.

Although *The Cheat*'s sordidness shocked Lasky to the point of almost rejecting it, DeMille convinced him that it would be worth making for the forward momentum it might give the Industry as a whole. At this early stage of film development, DeMille saw the necessity for pictures to deal with social questions of the day and to help provide answers to problems of prejudice and lawlessness by "pointing out incidents that shouldn't happen."

Only C. B. could have given justice to two films simultaneously. From 9:00 A.M. to 5:00 P.M. he directed *The Cheat,* after which he retired to his office where his secretary served him dinner. He then lay down to rest till 8:00 P.M. when it was time to direct *The Golden Chance.* They would work on this until 2:00 or 3.00 A.M. Sometimes he would sleep the few in-between hours at his office, but the pictures were both finished on schedule.

Although reviews of *The Golden Chance* were mild, *The Cheat,* as C. B. had predicted, caused an uproar. It made stars of Sessue Hayakawa and Fannie Ward; the usual manner of doing things was later reversed when a stage play was made out of C. B.'s opus. A grand opera followed.

Clearly foreshadowing his later work, *The Cheat* was one of the first of the domestic dramas dealing with the upper crust in their own environment and with their own problems. DeMille presented the situation from their point of view without attempting to moralize. Critics praised it as "true to life," while others condemned it for the same reason. *The Cheat,* through its influence on the industry, presaged the postwar movie patterns and laid the groundwork for DeMille's social films.

DeMille's stand on wanting to produce *The Cheat* was significant in that it showed he had an extrasensory perception that made him aware of an approaching tidal wave of public taste long before anyone else, least of all the public itself, detected the faintest ripple. In the prewar screen world, people were heroes, heroines, villains and vamps, but DeMille knew that these types were not going to be held valid for any length of time. He felt that a new public was coming to see films; one which preferred qualities of courage and weakness, evil and good, which had been heretofore offered clearly separated, all mixed together in a potent cocktail of human fallibility.

Through the beginning of 1918, DeMille drove himself and turned out a great number of films to keep his company afloat: *Temptation* (1915), *Chimmie Fadden Out West, Trail of the Lonesome Pine* (1916), *The Heart of Nora Flynn, The Dream Girl, Joan the Woman* (1917), *A Romance of the Redwoods, The Little American, The Woman God Forgot, The Devil Stone* and *The Whispering Chorus* (1918).

Joan the Woman, which featured Geraldine Farrar as the saint who gave her life for France, was a milestone in DeMille's development as a creator. He followed close on the pioneering heels of D. W. Griffith's *Birth of a Nation* (1914), but not in imitation, nor in competition, but in a passionate desire to go beyond the limitations in his art.

This film was his *first* historical spectacle. Griffith, the father of film making, had shown what was possible.

"I like spectacles," C. B. admitted. "I like to paint on a large canvas. I like it when the critics say I do it well. But I spend more time working on dramatic construction than I do planning spec-

Geraldine Farrar strikes a petulant pose (The Woman God Forgot, *1917*).

Geraldine Farrar in The Woman God Forgot.

Mary Pickford, Charles Ogle (left), Elliott Dexter, and Tully Marshall (right) in Romance of the Redwoods.

tacular effects. I'm afraid those critics who see only another DeMille spectacle do not analyze very deeply. Perhaps that is why some critics' opinion of the public goes lower and lower every time I make a successful picture."

During the filming of this epic a behind-the-scenes struggle for power was going on. Adolph Zukor, who had been quite successful with his Famous Players Film Co., was made president when his company merged with the Jesse L. Lasky Feature Play Company. He did not get along with Sam Goldwyn, who was chairman of the board at the time, and demanded his resignation. DeMille, who tried to keep out of the controversy, was unhappy when Goldwyn finally made his exit because they had started out together.

In *Joan the Woman* DeMille first experimented with color and double exposures. Its panoramas of war scenes, the ritual-like dream effects, and a striking double exposure (Joan is in Charles VII's court pleading for soldiers to save France, while dim and shadowed figures of great knights in armor plunge over them all) caused critics to compare the film with Ince's *Civilization* (1916), "equaling but not surpassing it."

This picture cost $302,976.26 and earned $605,731.40. Although not a big percentage grosser, C. B. learned a great deal about working on a grand scale.

In two films of this period, *Romance of the Redwoods* and *The Little American,* DeMille worked with America's Sweetheart and its highest-paid star, Mary Pickford. There were no fireworks. Miss Pickford was rather awed and afraid of the man who was by then considered a "Movie Moses."

In the early part of 1918, DeMille directed *The Whispering Chorus,* in which he became more deeply involved than in any previous film. *Chorus* was a forerunner of the "psychological" film, in which conflict arose within the characters rather than in forces external to them.

It is the story of a man condemned to death for his own murder. To escape the consequences of thefts from the office where he works, John Tremble runs away, finds a corpse in a river, mutilates it to

Mary Pickford in Romance of the Redwoods.

make it unidentifiable, puts his clothes on it, with his papers in the pocket. Years later—his own face having been disfigured in a waterfront brawl—he is arrested and convicted of murdering John Tremble. No one will believe his true account of the affair except his wife, now happily married again and expecting a child, who will be illegitimate if she acknowledges that Tremble is still alive. For the child's sake, she yields to her lawyer's advice that, even if the condemned man is indeed Tremble, he will surely be convicted of murdering the man whose body he dressed in his own clothes. Tremble himself, moved at last by love for his wife, lets her believe that he is guilty and goes to his death after writing out a confession that "the law is vindicated—I killed John Tremble."

Randolph Bartlett wrote in *Photoplay Magazine,* in the days when it was still a valid publication, "This is supposed to be a non-star production but Raymond Hatton is the unmistakeable star in as brilliant a character study as the film ever produced."

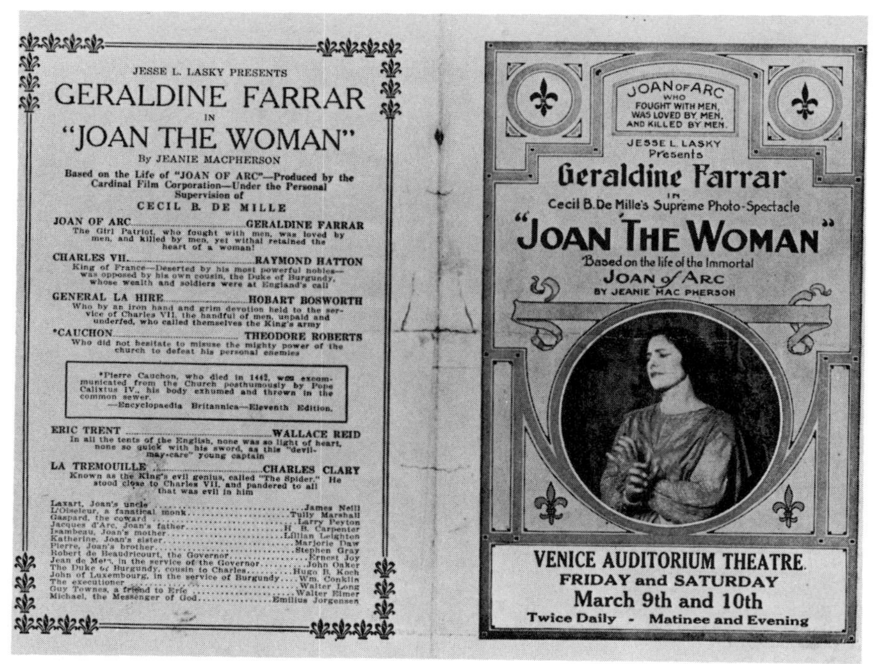

JESSE L. LASKY PRESENTS
GERALDINE FARRAR
IN
"JOAN THE WOMAN"
By JEANIE MACPHERSON

Based on the Life of "JOAN OF ARC"—Produced by the Cardinal Film Corporation—Under the Personal Supervision of
CECIL B. DE MILLE

JOAN OF ARC.................GERALDINE FARRAR
The Girl Patriot, who fought with men, was loved by men, and killed by men, yet withal retained the heart of a woman!

CHARLES VII.................RAYMOND HATTON
King of France—Deserted by his most powerful nobles—was opposed by his own cousin, the Duke of Burgundy, whose wealth and soldiers were at England's call

GENERAL LA HIRE.................HOBART BOSWORTH
Who by an iron hand and grim devotion held to the service of Charles VII, the handful of men, unpaid and underfed, who called themselves the King's army

*CAUCHON.................THEODORE ROBERTS
Who did not hesitate to misuse the mighty power of the church to defeat his personal enemies

*Pierre Cauchon, who died in 1442, was excommunicated from the Church posthumously by Pope Calixtus IV., his body exhumed and thrown in the common sewer.
—Encyclopaedia Britannica—Eleventh Edition.

ERIC TRENT.................WALLACE REID
In all the tents of the English, none was so light of heart, none so quick with his sword, as this "devil-may-care" young captain

LA TREMOUILLE.................CHARLES CLARY
Known as the King's evil genius, called "The Spider." He stood close to Charles VII, and pandered to all that was evil in him

Laxart, Joan's uncle.................James Neill
L'Oiseleur, a fanatical monk.................Tully Marshall
Gaspard, the coward.................Larry Peyton
Jacques d'Arc, Joan's father.................H. B. Carpenter
Isambeau, Joan's mother.................Lillian Leighton
Katherine, Joan's sister.................Marjorie Daw
Pierre, Joan's brother.................Stephen Gray
Robert de Beaudricourt, the Governor.................Ernest Joy
Jean de Metz, in the service of the Governor.................John Oaker
The Duke of Burgundy, cousin to Charles.................Hugo B. Koch
John of Luxembourg, in the service of Burgundy.................Wm. Conklin
The executioner.................Walter Long
Guy Townes, a friend to Eric.................Walter Elmer
Michael, the Messenger of God.................Emilius Jorgensen

JOAN OF ARC WHO FOUGHT WITH MEN, WAS LOVED BY MEN, AND KILLED BY MEN.
JESSE L. LASKY Presents
Geraldine Farrar
IN
Cecil B. De Mille's Supreme Photo-Spectacle
"JOAN THE WOMAN"
Based on the life of the Immortal
JOAN of ARC
BY JEANIE MAC PHERSON

VENICE AUDITORIUM THEATRE.
FRIDAY and SATURDAY
March 9th and 10th
Twice Daily - Matinee and Evening

A film program from Joan the Woman.

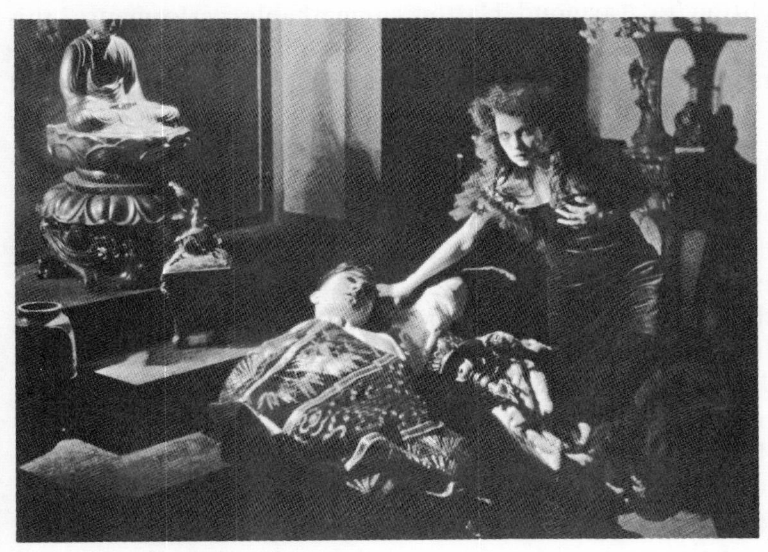

Scene from The Cheat *(1914).*

Raymond Hatton surrounded by "The Whispering Chorus," 1918.

In addition to Raymond Hatton's remarkable performance, this film was noteworthy because of the "chorus of faces," which gave the film its name. To show the thoughts struggling in the troubled mind of John Tremble, various faces—kindly, sullen, tempting, laughing, accusing, encouraging—were faded in and out, around his figure on the screen, as if they were speaking to him what he himself was thinking. For its time, this was an outstanding feat of photography, accomplished by double and multiple exposures. As Randolph Bartlett completed his review: "The final scenes are unnecessarily terrible; with awful, subtle suggestions that will drive sensitive spectators almost into hysterics. Much of the tale, however, has been splendidly told with the shadow representatives of silent voices handled in a manner most artistic."

The Whispering Chorus, which DeMille came to love like a bastard child, failed at the box office because it was too thought-provoking. It demanded too much intellectual participation from audiences. The film's failure was like a crown of thorns for DeMille: "I have been betrayed; I can never be hurt again."

But time proved him wrong. He loved his creations too much. That love was to betray him again, years later.

3

The bathroom became a mystical shrine ...

"Disgusting debauchery . . . most immoral episodes."

"It at least shows that the photoplay is breaking away from the marshmallow school of the drama."

"Classy . . . but rough in spots."

"A splendid story . . . faultlessly produced, carrying a powerful sermon."

Thus the 1918 critics barraged DeMille's first venture into the so-called social drama with *Old Wives for New.* Laying bare the lazy and slovenly wife of a meticulous and sensitive husband, it showed a side of marriage not even previously hinted at in movies. Had the Academy Awards been in existence, Sylvia Ashton would have won an Oscar for her loathsome performance, as she house-slippered through her day of littered abandon.

And to Elliott Dexter goes the dubious honor of having appeared in DeMille's first bathroom scene. As the wronged husband, he was shown trying to shave in a messy bathroom with dirty clothes scattered everywhere. One could hardly blame him for eventually falling in love with the beautiful, trim and fastidious Florence Vidor. Although no written censorship code had forbidden use of the bathroom, moviemakers shied away from the privy as a "matter of good taste." C. B. showed it too could become a prop.

By this time, Lasky Famous Players Company had two scenario departments, one in New York and one in Hollywood. Naturally, there was a healthy rivalry between them and *Old Wives for New* had been a bone of contention until DeMille demanded they let him produce it or sell it to another studio.

C.B. surrounded by Wallace Reid, Gloria Swanson, Elliott Dexter, and Theodore Kosloff on the set of The Affairs of Anatol.

DeMille with Gloria Swanson and Thomas Meighan, two of the actors he raised to stardom.

Sylvia Ashton on stairs in Old Wives for New *(1918.)*

Jesse Lasky settled it with a wire from New York: "I am strongly of the opinion that you should get away from the spectacle stuff for a couple more pictures and continue to do modern stories of great human interest."

When New York saw the finished product, eyebrows were raised and warning signals flashed. DeMille was so furious he took a print to a theatre in a nearby small town and asked the manager if he'd run it one afternoon without an announcement or rental fee. Quite by accident the "preview" was thus born. The result was quite exciting. The manager reported that before the picture was half through, sections of the audience had left, returning shortly with husbands, wives, or girl and boy friends. He had to screen it several times to accommodate the night crowds.

Although C. B. had made his point, he remained at odds with the New York scenario department because of their more conservative approach to films. On one occasion, having decided to put New York to a test, DeMille had his secretary, Gladys Rosson, copy word for word the script of a picture that had already done well at the box-

Wanda Hawley and Elliott Dexter in Old Wives for New.

office. Giving it another title he had Gladys's sister submit it to the New York story department as an original screenplay. It was returned as "unsuitable for filming."

Old Wives for New was the first of a series of modern comedies produced between 1918 and 1923 in which DeMille catered to the postwar trend toward higher living, heavier drinking and looser morals. Dwelling on both the desireability and foibles of the rich, he opened up a whole new world for the films, a world that middle-class audiences, newly won to the movies by the luxurious theaters then springing up, very much wanted to see.

DeMille turned out a dozen pictures which celebrated the dawn of the Jazz Age, relishing the sybaritic opulence of the world of fashion and the new freedom from moral restraints. He created a world in which people, charming and likeable people, did dangerous, reckless, even foolish, but always exciting things against a background of luxury, the flouting of convention and the hedonistic scramble for wealth and pleasure. His formula might have worked in any era: people have always been attracted by such daydreams. It was De-

Elliott Dexter in outdoor scene for We Can't Have Everything *(1918).*

Till I Come Back to You *(1918).*

Jack Holt, Elliott Dexter in The Squaw Man.

Mille's peculiar insight that the strait-laced Puritanism of prewar days was weakening and needed only to be given lip service to be placated. He dedicated his pictures to showing, at length and in intimate detail, what they ought *not* to do. The titles of his films left no doubt at all where his sympathies were.

Apart from Griffith, DeMille became the best known and most successful director of the era. And no small part of his success lay in his shrewd ability to change with and prophetically reflect the times.

What followed was not social but topical. Adapted by Bill DeMille from a novel by Rupert Hughes, it was titled *We Can't Have Everything*. Its hero was a movie director, who was a combination of C. B. himself and D. W. Griffith. Tully Marshall played the role so convincingly that DeMille felt he was seeing himself in several episodes, but insisted jokingly that "it was Griffith Tully imitated in the crazy scenes."

The climax was to be the burning down of a studio. But Lasky, believing it too expensive to build a convincing set, insisted they had to change the ending. DeMille, who usually scoffed at expense in favor of quality, reluctantly agreed but was unable to visualize another finish equally as strong. The solution came in form of an accident. Returning one day from location in Griffith Park, the company was shocked to see clouds of smoke rising near their film factory. To their amazement, *their* studio was being consumed by flames.

Unwilling to allow the situation to be a total loss, C. B. ordered his cameraman, Alvin Wyckoff, to set up the cameras. Tully Marshall may have found it a bit rough to "act" in the face of a very real disaster, but DeMille's determination kept them moving and the scene was shot as originally written.

Damage to the studio was estimated at $100,000, but C. B. dismissed the loss as lightly as he could. He told Lasky on the phone: "We'll get it back with the picture. One thing is destroyed so that something new may be created. We have fared well enough through the crisis."

Although C. B. never considered himself a star-maker, his films certainly catapulted a great number to instant fame and popularity. Tully Marshall became a matinee favorite following his performance in *We Can't Have Everything* (1918), in the same way that Wally Reid, Sessue Hayakawa, and Ray Hatton had.

Lew Cody gets ready for a romantic evening with Gloria Swanson in Don't Change Your Husband.

Elliott Dexter is Gloria Swanson's dinner date in this scene from Don't Change Your Husband.

A typical DeMille spectacle. Gloria Swanson swings above a rose-petaled pool in Don't Change Your Husband.

A family scene from For Better For Worse *(1919). L. to r.: Wanda Hawley, Mae Giraci, Elliott Dexter, and Gloria Swanson.*

Elliott Dexter seems to be interested in Mae Giraci; Gloria Swanson seems to be bored (For Better For Worse).

Lila Lee and Thomas Meighan in Male and Female *(1919).*

DeMille's greatest screen personality creation, however, was undoubtedly Gloria Swanson. After a number of minor parts in Sennett and Keystone comedies, she made her first credited appearance in C. B.'s *Don't Change Your Husband* (1918) followed immediately by *For Better or Worse;* but it was *Male and Female,* adapted in 1919 from Sir James Barrie's classic *The Admirable Crichton,* which put the tail on Miss Swanson's comet. Her bathtub scene in this film is the most memorable thing about it, for just as C. B. had introduced the bathroom to the screen, he now glamorized the bath itself.

When C. B. went into production in mid-1919 on that history-making bath scene, it was the first time that security guards had been placed around a Hollywood set. Everyone not performing a vital function was barred from the stage. After all, it had taken DeMille several days to convince the twenty-year-old budding actress to go through with it, and he didn't want any curious staring to make her feel ill at ease.

Draped in a silk towelette trimmed with yards of fringe, Gloria

Butler Tommy Meighan flirts with maid Lila Lee in Male and Female.

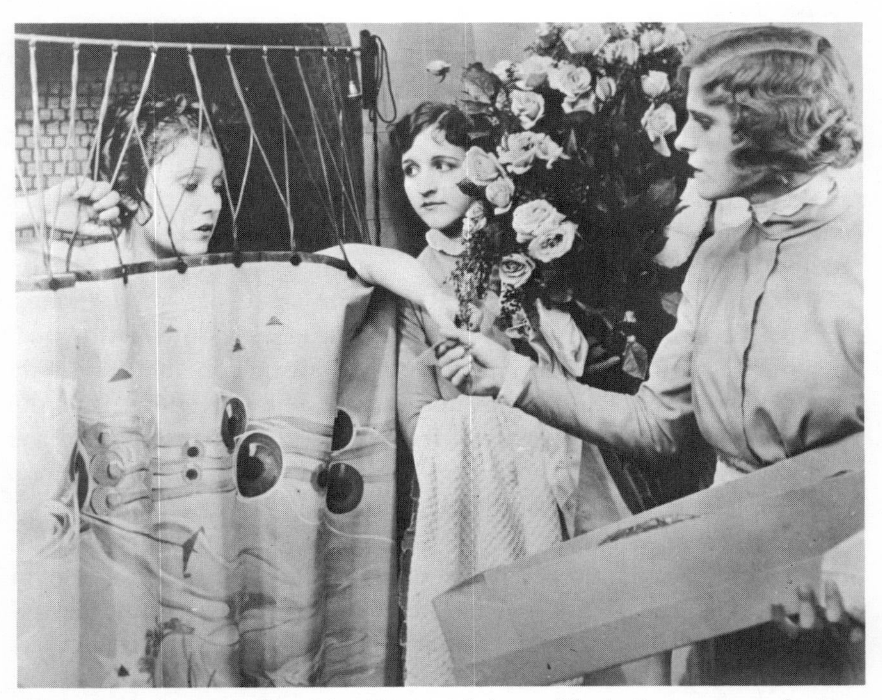

Julia Faye (l.) and Edna Mae Cooper (r.) get Gloria Swanson ready for a night out in Male and Female.

Gloria Swanson gets ready for a shower while Julia Faye and Edna Mae Cooper watch.

Swanson tripped into the spacious bathroom glowing with embarrassed expectancy. The gleaming sunken tub was flanked by two maids. When C. B. nodded, Julia Faye deftly lifted the towelette from her shoulders and Gloria eased into the rosewater, the camera focused on her bare upper back.

"Prolong it!" shouted C. B. "Relish the smell of the rosewater. More rapture; make the fans feel like they are going down with you." Back out of the water she came, into the waiting robe held by Julia Faye. And once again, after drying herself, she descended into the pool-like tub. Several repetitions relaxed her apprehensions and she began to smile, to enjoy her unpracticed enticement of the camera. Thus was the bath scene christened.

From then on, whatever the story of a DeMille film of the twenties, there came an obligatory halt in the plot for a lingering scene in which the heroine, sometimes the hero, washed and anointed herself in preparation for a gay masquerade ball or perhaps for some less public pleasure.

C. B. made of the bathroom a delightful resort which undoubtedly had its effects upon bathrooms across the nation. After generations

It's amazing that Thomas Meighan hasn't cut himself in this scene from Why Change Your Wife? *That thought seems not to have occurred to Bebe Daniels.*

A cast of characters in Why Change Your Wife? *L. to r.: Theodore Kosloff, Sylvia Ashton, Thomas Meighan, Gloria Swanson, and Bebe Daniels.*

of Puritanism, it was thrilling to be told that bodily beauties were not a shame nor a weakness. American bathrooms, previously severely utilitarian, took on the gleam of marble, tile and chrome, and the tactile luxury of great fuzzy towels and rugs. By the end of the decade, plumbing corporations, which had never dared mention their wares in public, were taking full-page ads in newspapers and magazines displaying bathroom fixtures frankly modeled on the DeMille splendor. (C. B.'s home bathrooms, however, remained utilitarian.)

The bath became a mystical shrine dedicated to the gods, and the art of bathing was shown as a ceremony rather than merely a sanitary duty. Undressing was not just the removing of clothes, but a progressive revelation of entrancing beauty, a study in diminishing draperies. The point was that in no stage of dress or undress need a woman look unlovely. To this end, underclothes became visions of translucent promise and nightgowns silken sensuality and invitation.

After the bathroom and the bath, the bedroom was DeMille's next choice for cinematic emphasis. Here too disrobing and enrobing

Bebe Daniels and Thomas Meighan in Why Change Your Wife?

Elliott Dexter shows tender concern for the welfare of Gloria Swanson in Something to Think About.

Gloria Swanson, Elliott Dexter, and Julia Faye in Something to Think About.

Forrest Stanley and Agnes Ayres rendezvous in Forbidden Fruit, *1921.*

Clarence Burton makes quiet exit before concerned Agnes Ayres and puzzled Theodore Roberts in Forbidden Fruit.

Clarence Burton and Winter Hall read this important message; Theodore Kosloff is an interested spectator (Forbidden Fruit).

was carried on at length and in full view of the camera. The romantic glory of the bed later culminated in a film called *The Golden Bed* in 1925. DeMille's beds were things to dream about, constructed more for art, culture, love-making and style, than for sleep.

C. B. went far beyond the now classic bath scene with Gloria Swanson in the making of *Male and Female*. His was a rather free adaptation of Barrie's story about an English noble family who are shipwrecked on an island and saved by the butler who takes command. True, it was a snide barb at British class snobbery, and the story had enough action and excitement, but DeMille got the urge to hypo it with a strain of eroticism.

He added a Babylonian flashback without consulting Sir James Barrie. Also without Sir James's consent, C. B. had changed the title from *The Admirable Crichton* to *Male and Female*. What had inspired the new title was the strong objection raised by the New York publicity and sales departments, which insisted that the public rarely encountered the word "admirable" and would confuse it with "admiral." Consequently, they would stay away from it under the false impression that it was a naval picture. For some unaccountable reason, sea movies weren't popular at that particular time.

When Lasky had called about the snag, DeMille vexed aloud, "I'll give them a title they'll like." After pondering overnight, he announced with a trace of sarcasm, "We'll call it *Male and Female.* I guess the sales department and public will understand that." They understood, and the picture went out under the more provocative title.

Jesse Lasky, by a strange coincidence, happened to be making a trip to London on the same boat that was carrying the first print of *Male and Female* to be sent overseas. George Graham, his general manager in England, was relieved to see him and was quick to point out that their contract with Barrie contained a clause obliging them to show him the film adaptations of his plays before releasing them in Great Britain. Graham passed the hot potato to Lasky.

A screening of the picture was set up for Sir James in a private projection room. Lasky was the only other person present; Graham

Wallace Reid and Wanda Hawley share a tender moment in The Affairs of Anatol *(1921).*

Gloria Swanson (l.) and Bebe Daniels seem to be preparing for a showdown (The Affairs of Anatol).

Bebe Daniels in the Affairs of Anatol.

John Davidson, Mildred Harris, and Conrad Nagel in Fool's Paradise *(1922).*

Mildred Harris in the ballet sequence of Fool's Paradise.

Conrad Nagel and John Davidson in Fool's Paradise.

had begged off. Barrie spoke up, "I've been looking forward to seeing *The Admirable Crichton* for some time."

Lasky shuddered. He wanted to burrow down into the upholstery of his projection room seat, but he knew that he had to break the news before Barrie saw it on the screen. "Sir James, it's a . . . that is . . . I mean it is a fine picture," he stammered. "It wasn't my idea, but you see, sir, the American idiom isn't exactly the King's English, and our director, Cecil DeMille, is a very determined and sometimes difficult man. And . . . well . . . he decided to call it *Male and Female.*"

The dead silence, during which Lasky had expected the heavens to fall, as in "Chicken Little," Graham had feared, was broken by Barrie's exclamation, "Capital. Wish I'd thought of it myself."

Twenty years later, critic Lewis Jacobs, in a retrospective and analytic look at this film hailed it for its revolutionary treatment of sex and its establishment of DeMille as a pace-setting director of the early post-war years.

It was at this point that C. B. was attracted to his first picture, *The Squaw Man*, and he became the first director to re-make a

Julia Faye, Conrad Nagel, and John Davidson at a masquerade ball in Saturday Night.

Conrad Nagel and Edith Roberts in Saturday Night.

picture. The second version enjoyed even greater success than the first. Then in 1931, he filmed a third version, this one in sound, making DeMille the only man to produce the same film three times successfully.

During this period besides the above-mentioned films, DeMille produced *Till I Come Back to You* (1918), *Why Change Your Wife?* (1920), *Something to Think About, Forbidden Fruit* (1921), *The Affairs of Anatol, Fool's Paradise* (1922) and *Saturday Night.*

DeMille's name came to mean as much to success at the box-office as Mary Pickford or Douglas Fairbanks. Like Griffith, DeMille felt quality was what he wanted more than anything else. In December of 1920, the *Motion Picture News,* released the following prophetic quote in a story about the new cinema Caesar:

"Barely six years ago I made fourteen pictures in a single year. . . . Today, working just as hard or harder, I find that I can only turn out three pictures in the same length of time. But the three pictures that I make today draw more patronage than the entire fourteen of six years ago. It is not beyond the bounds of reason to say that the picture of the future may take a year or more to produce."

In 1922, he completed only two films, *Fool's Paradise* and *Saturday Night.* The latter was outstanding for its use of a massive swimming pool scene that climaxed a wild party.

Julia Faye recalled what could have been a most embarrassing mishap: "My bathing suit was made of big squares of patent leather, it was quite effective, reflecting the lanterns hung around the pool. There was a large group dancing in and around the pool. Suddenly in the middle of the take, I felt something snap. A young extra standing beside me realized my calamity and quickly hugged me so that I couldn't be seen. When C. B. shouted Cut! I saw the storm signals as he rushed over wanting to know what was going on. I told him he should thank this young man. He saved me from an awful embarrassment. My suit came apart when I hit the water and I lost half the top."

DeMille simmered down and shook the young man's hand for using his head and not spoiling the scene by shouting that Miss Faye was in the all-together. "By the way, what's your name, young fellow?"

"William Boyd, sir," the extra replied. And C. B. took an immediate fancy to his easy smile and made himself a mental note to use him in a later picture in a more prominent role.

Critics have called this period DeMille's divorce-marriage decade,

Edith Roberts, Jack Mower, Leatrice Joy, and Conrad Nagel in Saturday Night.

First indoor mixed pool party (Saturday Night).

Leatrice Joy, Julia Faye, and John Davidson in all their regalia (Saturday Night).

also citing it as his "production-conscious cycle." Indeed, clothes, furniture, makeup, lighting and props were nearly as important to DeMille as his actors. His qualitative concern for detail led many to believe that he was just too "thing-conscious."

Continued complete attention by DeMille to something like clothes made the public very aware of them. They in turn put more emphasis on how and what dresses should be worn and where. C. B. made Gloria Swanson his female clothes-horse, setting and turning fashion trends. Although at this time only a fair actress, DeMille's use of her made her one of the big attractions of the twenties. DeMille also cast young white-haired Bill Boyd as a male clothes horse because he had an extensive wardrobe.

C. B.'s glamorization of beds and bathrooms led to new movements in interior decorating. These commonplace rooms were no longer merely functional, but showcases—the most elaborately adorned rooms in the house.

DeMille and Adolph Zukor in 1919 Locomobile in front of Lasky Studio on Vine Street.

Director DeMille went about the business of giving "style" to films; and, to a great degree, he was successful. But he had not yet learned to use his camera as an artist's tool and still regarded it as a mere reproducing instrument. Still caught up in intricate theatrics, he thought of films not as a fluid medium, but as a series of separate pictures. Although his illustrations were on a grand scale and as perfect as he could make them, his films lacked a cinematic continuity, a failing only partly compensated for by sensual diversions. When he was finally able to change his basic conception of moving pictures, his style improved remarkably.

As for his ability to direct actors, one contemporary said that he was "lacking in Griffith's demoniac faculty of making an extra do in a picture just what he would do in life." A feat which was later credited to C. B. also.

In an interview in 1922, DeMille said that he believed in having actors play their parts without outlining every grimace, every gesture for them. He liked, and was usually able to get, spontaneity. Nevertheless, he was noted for being "all over the set," stopping the camera to illustrate an action himself. It was said he seemed to draw the work out of the players by the force of his personality.

With open-throat shirt, puttees, Louis XV hat, a drooping pipe, a silver whistle and silver bugle, Cecil B. DeMille strode across the early twenties' Hollywood landscape like a colossus, establishing an extravagant prototype of the film director.

4

"You cannot break the Ten Commandments . . ."

"Jeanie, will you go to jail for your art?"

Jeanie MacPherson, actress turned writer, smiled at C. B. remembering his sense of humor. But seeing the furrows in his brow, she tried to match his mood.

"If you say so, sir."

So Jeanie MacPherson went to Detroit, stole a fur piece by prearrangement from a friend, was arrested with the goods on her and sentenced to jail. Three days later, a police official, who knew the circumstances, obtained her release. She returned with enough notes about "being barred" to make five movies.

Thus atmosphere and facts for *Manslaughter* (1922), a drama of a speed-crazy girl who kills a motorcycle officer and is sent to prison by the District Attorney who loves her, was authenticated. Leatrice Joy and Thomas Meighan played the leads.

In *Manslaughter,* DeMille used his second flashback to ancient times—the fall of Rome and the coming of the Goths! A shocking rape and orgy scene was daringly paralleled with the sensation-seekers that would destroy America if tolerated. The film was an instant smash.

But when he experimented with a third flashback, this time to prehistoric times for *Adam's Rib* (1923), the critics blasted him. E. V. Durling: "A dangerous conception of social life." C. Ruth Doran: "The silly weak story it told did not satisfy such expenditure. In other words, there was much ado about nothing."

DeMille, who had heard much good from the critics before, was dismayed at their bitter dislike for *Adam's Rib*. Perhaps he thought

Milton Sills, Pauline Garon, and Theodore Kosloff in prehistoric wardrobe for Adam's Rib, *1923.*

DeMille goes to sea. More notes for his secretary, Gladys Rosson, at the end of the day. (The work was on The Ten Commandments, *silent version.)*

Leatrice Joy pleads woefully with Lois Wilson in Manslaughter, *1922.*

A talented partnership between Thomas Meighan and Leatrice Joy (Manslaughter).

Leatrice Joy dreams of bacchanalia.

View of the largest exterior set ever built for a motion picture. It was used in the biblical prologue of C.B.'s production for Paramount, The Ten Commandments, *1923.*

Completed exterior: This is a reproduction of the city which Pharaoh Rameses II forced the Children of Israel to build to his glory. It broke the record formerly held by the "Robin Hood" castle. It was 750 feet wide and 109 feet high, and it was approached by an avenue of 24 sphinxes.

DeMille, Estelle Taylor, and Jeanie MacPherson confer on set of Ten Commandments.

Cameras aboard fast-flying cars are being prepared to be "out in front" when 250 chariots, 500 horses, and 500 men started on the most spectacular chariot charge in 3000 years. The scenes were shot on the famous Muroc Dry Lake, Mojave Desert, California—an expanse of over 100 square miles as flat as a hardwood floor.

they were right, and he sought to find out. The only way to do that was to go to the people who went to movies and ask them what they wanted to see. He launched a huge contest, offering $1000 for the best idea for a picture.

Letters, wires and calls came in from all over the country. Suggestions ranged in subject from the "most sacred to the most profane." The celebrated director was impressed by the great number who wanted a religious theme, and there was one suggestion that kept coming back to C. B.'s mind as he sifted through the mountain of envelopes. It had come from a manufacturer of lubricating oil in Lansing, Michigan, whose name was F. C. Nelson. He had begun his letter with: "You cannot break the Ten Commandments—they will break you!"

Seven others had submitted the same idea and C. B. awarded each with $1000 and launched *The Ten Commandments* (1923), his greatest cinema adventure. As he conceived it, his film would have to be significant to contemporary audiences and he decided to tell in a prologue the liberation of the Hebrew from Egypt and the acquisition of the ten commandments by Moses on the mountain top;

Estelle ("Miriam") Taylor leads the revelers in the Golden Calf orgies.

The Israelites at the Red Sea.

Moses (Theodore Roberts) condemns the erring Jews.

Estelle Taylor worships the Golden Calf.

Moses receives the Ten Commandments.

Rod La Rocque and Nita Naldi in love scene from the "modern" sequence of The Ten Commandments.

Rod La Rocque, Leatrice Joy, and Richard Dix.

Richard Dix reads one of the commandments to an unhappy Leatrice Joy.

then to juxtapose this against a modern story of two brothers, one of whom lived by the commandments while the other broke them, climaxing in his consequent tragedy and the death of their mother.

When C. B. proposed this, his first film with a Biblical background, he was told: "Nobody wants to see people running around wearing bedsheets." He went ahead anyway, and after he had spent over $1 million and still wasn't finished, New York sent word that "You must have lost your mind. Suspend production immediately."

Not willing to abandon the project, DeMille offered to sell everything he owned and buy the picture. It was an unprecedented act of faith and he was allowed to continue. A fact not well known is that C. B. donated every cent he made on this and on his later *King of Kings* (1927) to charity.

The parting of the Red Sea during the Exodus was the most inspiring moment in cinema history to that date. DeMille gave full credit to Roy Pomeroy of the Paramount special effects department. Dr. T. K. Peters, who assisted Pomeroy, described how it was done:

Onlookers watch curiously after the collapse of the church. In front, l. to r.: Richard Dix, Edythe Chapman, Charles Ogle, Rod La Rocque.

Rod La Rocque indulges in a little bit of editing in these two scenes from Triumph.

Lillian Rich relaxes on The Golden Bed.

"A huge bank of gelatin was molded on top of a table so constructed that it was equipped with scores of small gas jets. The gelatin was parted in the middle, the jets were ignited, and as the gelatin melted and flowed together, churned by the force of the jets, two cameras shot the scene. The film was then reversed and shots of the Israelites crossing dry land and Egyptians getting engulfed were double exposed on this scene."

This special effects achievement was repeated in DeMille's second version of *The Ten Commandments* thirty years later. General feeling indicated, however, that the first parting of the Red Sea far surpassed the second.

DeMille's expense on *The Ten Commandments* was justified in the film's overwhelming reception by the public and critics alike.

Lillian Rich chooses elegant evening dress in The Golden Bed.

Lillian Rich poses as a most unusually dressed bride.

C.B. discusses scene with Lillian Rich and monkey actor.

William Boyd from The Volga Boatman *(1926)*

DeMille directing The Volga Boatman.

William Boyd and Victor Varconi in The Volga Boatman.

The three stars of Volga Boatman *in tender moment.*

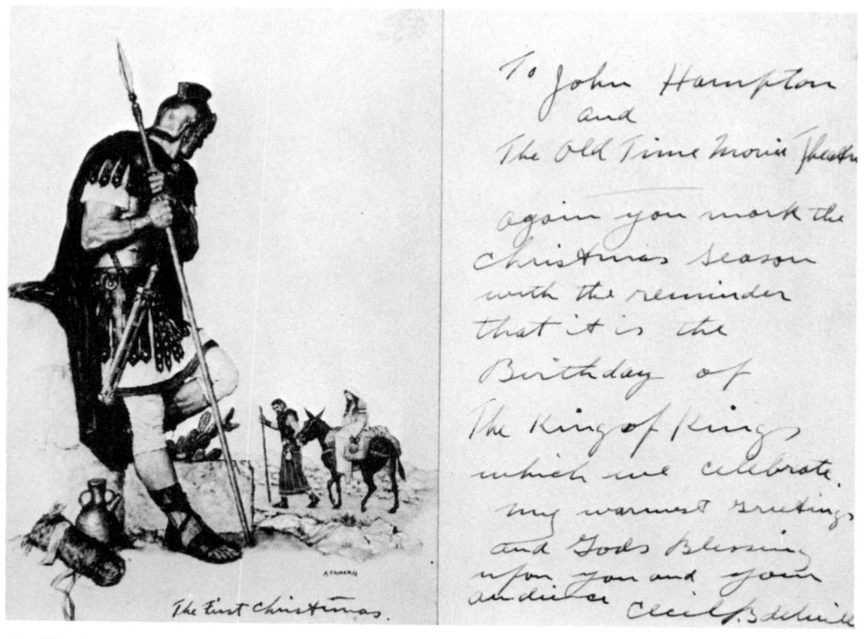

The First Christmas.

To John Hampton
and
The Old Time Movie Theatr

again you mark the
Christmas Season
with the reminder
that it is the
Birthday of
The King of Kings
which we celebrate.
my warmest greetings
and Gods Blessing
upon you and your
audience
Cecil B. deMille

A Christmas greeting in DeMille's handwriting to John Hampton, who for 25 years has run the Silent Movie Theater in Hollywood.

This old advertisement demonstrates the enduring popularity of the name of DeMille.

Many tributes piled on his desk, but DeMille treasured one above all—a congratulatory note from David Belasco, the immortal stage-genius who had worked closely with DeMille's father and under whom C. B. had started his career as an actor. This film was the first of DeMille's mammoth spectacles that were to be forever associated with his name. Ever afterwards, the moral tone of his pictures was lofty, though it was never allowed to detract from display and sexuality.

Aware of the terrific letdown that follows a major success because of the inability to sustain the feeling of euphoria for any length of time, C. B. plunged himself right into another film, *Triumph* (1924). Probably made more modest by comparison to the picture that immediately preceded it, this film enjoyed only minor celebra-

DeMille chats with cameraman Pev Marley on set of King of Kings.

tion. And then with *Feet of Clay* (1924), C. B., "still searching for the Divine," attempted an exploration of the hereafter and was slashed by the critics for his "abortive failure to explain the ways of God."

The New York office became extremely concerned with the increasing amount of money spent on DeMille's films—a cost that C. B. did not share because he drew his salary from 50 percent of the gross, not the profits. New York finally urged him in 1924 to return to social films, thinking that contemporary stories would curtail his spending. His next film, *The Golden Bed,* which had a spectacular candy ball and ballet, received great patronage but still had a high budget.

The question of finances, which had been a burr to the company

New York City's Gaiety Theatre in 1927, when King of Kings *opened.*

Mickey Moore as Mark leads blind girl, Muriel McCormick, to Christ in King of Kings.

H. B. Warner as Christ with apostle Joseph Striker. The boy is played by Mickey Moore and Ernest Torrance is Peter.

Jacqueline Logan as Mary Magdalene in The King of Kings.

Mary Magdalene, played by Jacqueline Logan, rides to face Christ (The King of Kings).

Joseph Schildkraut as Judas and Jacqueline Logan as Mary (The King of Kings).

H. B. Warner with Julia Faye. (l.) as Mary and Josephine Norman as Mary of Bethany.

for some time, was pushed to an explosive state in December 1924 by Sidney Kent, sales manager in New York, who, backed by Zukor, went to Lasky and insisted that readjustments in DeMille's contract be made. They wanted his salary to be part of the profits instead of the gross and to place severe limitations on his spending. The result of conferences between these three men and C. B. was the cancellation of his contract.

In recalling the final moments of their partnership, DeMille said: "There is no doubt in my mind that those three gentlemen believed they were acting in fairness to the company and to me, as firmly as I believed that the only way I could make good pictures was the way I had been making them. But my life has had few more bitter mo-

Mary Magdalene (Jacqueline Logan) is released from her sins.

H. B. Warner as Christ writes the sins of the onlookers in the sand as Majel Coleman, the adulteress, cowers before her accusers.

Christ is hailed by his followers.

Rudolph and Joseph Schildkraut, real-life father and son, play key roles of the High Priest Caiaphas and Judas in The King of Kings.

The Last Supper.

H. B. Warner (c.), Joseph Striker (l.), and Joseph Schildkraut (r.) at Last Supper.

Theodore Kosloff accuses Ernest Torrance of being a follower of Christ.

H. B. Warner before Pilate (Victor Varconi) and accused by Rudolph Schildkraut.

H. B. Warner on the road to Calvary.

H. B. Warner is aided by William Boyd as Simon of Cyrene.

ments than when Mr. Zukor said to me and the other two listened in unprotecting silences: 'Cecil, you have never been one of us.' "

C. B.'s first move as an independent was to buy the Thomas Ince Studios in Hollywood for $500,000 and rechristen it the DeMille Studio. In arranging for distribution of the pictures he hoped to make he was introduced to Jeremiah Milbank, a wealthy businessman who had recently formed the Producers Distributing Corporation. This was Milbank's first venture into the film industry, and being quite religious was drawn to C. B. when told of DeMille's dream, that of producing the life of Christ. Milbank agreed not only to distribute his films but to give full financial support to the project.

DeMille's initial productions for his own studio were two adventure stories, both of which featured William Boyd, the young extra he had employed as a clothes horse. *The Road to Yesterday* (1925) introduced Boyd as an actor to film goers and *The Volga Boatman* (1926) insured his stardom. C. B. had cranked out these two films in haste to get some capital rolling into the studio so that he could

The Crucifixion.

Earthquake scene as Christ dies on the Cross.

"Only to the Cross I cling!" Jacqueline Logan as Mary Magdalene at the Cross.

Rock rolls from Christ's tomb.

begin on what many believe to be his masterpiece, *The King of Kings.*

"All my life," C. B. said amid preparations, "I've wondered how many have been turned away from Christianity by the effeminate, sanctimonious, machine-made Christ of Sunday school books. The Christ was actually a man with a body hard enough to withstand 40 days of fasting and long journeys on foot and nights of sleepless prayer, a man with a mind razor sharp, whose ranging thoughts measured the kingdoms of the world against the lilies in the field, a man who had compassion for sinners, and unleashed His anger and biting scorn only on the hypocrites who made a travesty of His father's temple. There could well have been a note of admiration in the voice of Pilate when he said of Him: 'Behold the Man!' "

There was only one man DeMille knew who could play Christ: H. B. Warner. "He understood perfectly well how I wanted Him portrayed," said C. B. "He had all the virility, tenderness, authority yet restraint, compassion tempered with strength, touch of gentle humor, enjoyment of small and simple things, a divine love of his brethren and enemies alike that the Man of Nazareth must have had."

That C. B. had been right about Warner was confirmed years later by a minister who told the actor, "I saw you in *The King of Kings* as a child, and now, everytime I speak of Jesus, it is your face I see."

When DeMille left Lasky Famous Players Co., scores of technicians and production people followed him—including Jeanie MacPherson, who had a major hand in scripting *King of Kings.* Brother Bill resigned from Lasky and joined C. B. in 1926.

Throughout the filming, a Jesuit priest from the Federal Council of Churches, and another member of the clergy were present to give advice. Extraordinary steps were taken (and publicized) to insure a proper attitude of reverence. H. B. Warner in costume as Christ was spoken to by no one save the director, who arranged for the actor to be veiled and transported in a closed car. Besides having his meals in solitude on location, Warner was also instructed not to be seen in public during production. The first day of shooting started with the uttering of prayers by representatives of Protestant, Catholic, Jewish, Buddhist and Moslem faiths. And on that day DeMille used an electric speaker system to direct crowd scenes for the first time.

The film itself shows DeMille at his best, and at his worst. C. B. gave some insight into his unique ability to combine piety with richly commercial paradings of sex and sadism: "I decided to jolt them all out of their preconceptions with an opening scene that none of them would be expecting, a lavish party in the luxurious home of Mary Magdalene. This beautiful courtesan is surrounded by the leering, sensual faces of her admirers who taunt her because one of their number, young Judas, evidently found the company of some wandering carpenter more interesting."

Years later, in his autobiography, DeMille wrote that his most moving experience as a film director came the evening when he called the final "Cut!" on this picture—it was a scene of the Crucifixion. As the players started to leave the set, he raised his hands and spoke: "It is Christmas Eve, the birthday of our Saviour, and we have just finished recreating His death. I want you, if you will, to think about that for just a minute. I'm going to ask the organist to play. If you are in the habit of praying, you may want to pray, if not just consider what the significance is of what we have just seen, and what is best and highest in life for you."

The organ played and there was a little movement from the back of the stage toward the three crosses. Some dropped to their knees,

Lina Basquette in Godless Girl *(1928).*

George Duryea, Lina Basquette in Godless Girl.

Marie Prevost braces for a beating from the sadistic matron of Godless Girl.

This scene from Godless Girl *shows Lina Basquette in the title role and George Duryea as the hero, after their escape from the reformatory. Once bitter enemies, mutual interests have brought them together and their escape develops into romance.*

Marie Prevost and Lina Basquette in Godless Girl.

Lina Basquette and George Duryea in Godless Girl.

Feet of Clay *(1924). L. to r.: Julia Faye, Rod La Rocque, Vera Reynolds, Ricardo Cortez, William Boyd (far right), Robert Edeson (standing in background).*

William Boyd and Rod La Rocque in Feet of Clay.

End of an orgy in Manslaughter *(1922).*

making the sign of the cross. A few wept freely. And after several minutes, the area slowly emptied without a word.

The King of Kings premiered in New York on April 19, 1927, to unbelievably large crowds. To date, it is estimated that over 8 billion people throughout the world have seen the picture. The film so touched Milbank that he joined C. B. in donating all proceeds to charity.

A moving picture of such impact could not avoid setting off violent controversies. To DeMille's fury, the film was banned in many American cities because Jewish organizations claimed it condemned the Jewish people as the crucifiers of Christ. DeMille went to great lengths to show that only a few corrupt religious leaders demanded Christ's death, and had even made Caiaphas rather than Judas responsible for Christ's death in the film to soften Jewish susceptibilities, but he failed to convince them.

In appraising *King of Kings,* critic Laurence Reid commended DeMille's courage for departing from conventions and presenting Christ as a flesh and blood man: "Heretofore, it has been held as

Leatrice Joy in climactic scene from Manslaughter. *Dog star Teddy is passenger.*

Joseph Schildkraut and Jetta Goudal are caught between trains in The Road to Yesterday.

William Boyd and Vera Reynolds in The Road to Yesterday, *(1925).*

sacrilegious to depict Christ carrying the cross to Calvary. But DeMille handles the scene so reverently that any thought of trespassing on sacred ground cannot be encouraged. There will be some who smirk over the picture because of some past exotic gesture from Cecil's Italian hand. . . . Even though not a greatly inspired film, it will create an emotional experience for all who see it. With religionists, it will find heartiest enthusiasm. As for those who are far from spiritual maturity, it will kindle a finer humanity. Thus it will serve its purpose—beyond its being a work of art—to awaken faith."

For almost thirty years, hundreds of stories crossed DeMille's desk about how the picture influenced the lives of people all over the world. One such story was told him by a German minister, Pastor H. E. Wallner.

Scene from The Road to Yesterday.

Elliott Dexter in Adam's Rib *(1923).*

Dinosaur skeletons steal the scene from Elliot Dexter and Pauline Garon (Adams Rib).

Elliott Dexter and Julia Faye in caveman scene from Adam's Rib.

As a young man in Danzig in 1928, Wallner went to see *The King of Kings* because he was a fan of Joseph Schildkraut's. He was so moved by the picture that he decided to devote his life to the ministry of the Lutheran Church. He had a parish in Prague when Hitler marched on Czechoslovakia. In his congregation was a doctor, a Jewish convert to Christianity, who was thrown into a concentration camp where his example and encouragement to the other prisoners to die bravely, with faith in their hearts, so angered the Gestapo officers that they beat him with an iron rod until one of his arms was so badly smashed that it had to be amputated.

"One of the greatest rewards of my career," said DeMille in retrospect a few months before his death, "was realized when that good pastor told me, 'If it were not for *The King of Kings,* I would not be a Lutheran pastor, and three hundred and fifty Jewish children would have died in the ditches."

John Hampton, owner and manager of the Silent Movie Theatre on Fairfax Boulevard in Hollywood, where he shows only silent films, tells another curious tale about *King of Kings:* "We ran it at Christmastime the first year we were open in 1942. It was the most popular film we had. About 1952, after running it every year at Christmas, we decided to give the picture a rest. You couldn't believe the complaints, phone calls and telegrams, all to the effect that we'd ruined the year by not ending it with *King of Kings.*

"There was such an uproar that it got written up in the papers. The following year, we didn't make that mistake again, and advertised it. DeMille, who had a sentimental interest in the film, must have seen an ad because he sent us a Christmas card noting that he was pleased that we were showing it again. He also sent over a large basket of two dozen white mums for the showing.

"DeMille was interested in keeping this particular film going. He used to put it into the Pantages Theatre on Hollywood Boulevard at Easter and admit people free. One of the things that kept *King of Kings* so timeless was the fact that so many of the scenes were static, like paintings by the masters. He told me that he patterned the sets and key scenes after famous art works."

True to form, C. B. didn't wait for the laurels to accumulate for *King of Kings* and began early in 1927 on *The Godless Girl,* a tale of high school atheist clubs. It told of a girl who goes from bad to worse, but is finally redeemed by gaining faith in God. The film, although interesting because of its expose of reformatories, was almost outdated before it was released. The screen had begun to speak and C. B.'s *Godless Girl* was caught in the middle. Some feet of soundtrack were added to the picture before it went into general distribution, but it was still a silent film.

C. B. was, of course, in no financial position to revamp his small studio with the latest in sound equipment. The depression had started and the purse strings held by Milbank in New York became so taut that DeMille Studio often had trouble meeting the payroll on time.

Unable to recoup enough financial backing to continue, DeMille sold his studio to Pathé, which was then owned by Joseph P. Kennedy, whose second son would become President. Then on August 28, 1928, C. B. signed a contract to make three pictures for MGM Studios. Taking his personal staff with him, he set up offices in a special bungalow on the Metro lot.

"Oh God, what I will be able to do with sound!" he exclaimed.

5

The turbulent transition from the silents to the talkies . . .

Cecil B. DeMille was one of the few producer-directors to survive the turbulent transition from the silents to the talkies.

For *Dynamite* (1929), his first talkie, he imported the fiery stage actor, Charles Bickford, for the lead, thus winning a long-term contract with MGM for Bickford. During the production of *Dynamite,* a threadbare melodrama, C. B. realized the need for a long-arm microphone boom and for a portable sound camera whose whirring wouldn't be picked up on the sound tracks; before completing the picture, he had contributed both to the advent of sound films.

His second for MGM was the only musical (and a feeble one at that), that he ever produced, *Madam Satan* (1930), in which his daughter Katherine made her debut. Then to complete his contract, C. B. produced *The Squaw Man* a third time. As his final MGM picture was readied for release, the stock market crashed and he lost over $1 million. *The Squaw Man,* too, suffered in the sudden onslaught of the depression and in the final balance showed $150,000 in the red. Yet by depression standards, it was a success.

"My three years at MGM were not particularly happy," said DeMille later. He could not agree with their production methods, nor they with his. Both were relieved when his contract expired.

Between 1913 and 1931, C. B.'s films cost, in round figures, about $12 million and had grossed $28 million; in consideration of this record Paramount Studios, which is what the Famous Players-Lasky Corporation was now called, invited DeMille back to make one picture, *The Sign of the Cross* (1932). They told him, "Remember Cecil, you're on trial with this picture," confirming the old

Mrs. DeMille, who made a habit of visiting her husband on the set for the first day's shooting of every one of his pictures, on the set of Union Pacific.

Hollywood adage that "You're only as good as your last picture," and C. B.'s last had failed to make a profit.

The financial crisis that had beset the country had severely rocked the power structure at Paramount. Lasky was on his way out, on a temporary leave of absence which was to last 25 years. And although Zukor was still in the president's chair, he was soon forced to vacate it, although still remaining in charge of production.

As some Jews had opposed *King of Kings,* many Catholics vehemently contested the morality of *Sign of the Cross,* which showed the triumph of their religion in the face of Roman persecutions. Their objections focalized on a dance sequence during an orgy which was intended to arouse the virginal heroine into sexual love with the Roman hero.

Will Hays, the self-appointed censorship director backed by Martin Quigley, publication king, called C. B. and asked, "What are you going to do about the dance?"

"Will," replied DeMille, "Listen carefully because you might want to quote me. Not a damn thing."

"Not a damn thing?" questioned Hays.

"Not a damn thing!" affirmed C. B.

DeMille later explained: "How are you going to resist temptation if there isn't any. That's what the dance was all about and the heroine's rejection was a triumph of virtue."

Indeed, it was impossible not to be impressed by the moralising of *Sign of the Cross,* no matter how much it was a melodrama of sex and violence played out against ornate backgrounds, even celebrating paganism. The opening scene, where Nero and his courtiers, seeming to float on a marble dais above the holocaust, look down with mingled excitement and horror at Rome burning beneath them, sets the style. It is continued by Frederic March's centurion

C.B. (l.) and Jesse Lasky, Jr. join Jeannie MacPherson for a birthday celebration.

DeMille, wearing hat, directly to left of camera, lines up on Lynne Overman, Gary Cooper, and Preston Foster for a scene in North West Mounted Police.

who thrashes his way through Roman crowds, driving them from his chariot wheels with a whip. As the dissolute Poppaea, Claudette Colbert easily matches Charles Laughton's simpering Nero, both of whom benefit from Mitchell Leisen's imaginative costumes.

As the stock market crash had probably kept *Squaw Man* from success, *Sign of the Cross* was threatened by the closing of the banks. The draw, however, of this film was so strong that people without cash, gave IOU's to theatre managers for admission. Nearly every note was redeemed when money was again in circulation.

Redeemed by the profits from *Sign of the Cross,* Paramount extended to DeMille a permanent office and greater freedom in production decisions. Following his next two pictures, *This Day and*

Charles Bickford and Kay Johnson in two scenes from Dynamite, *1929.*

Charles Bickford and a suave Conrad Nagel in Dynamite.

Conrad Nagel (l.) with Kay Johnson and Charles Bickford in Dynamite.

Kay Johnson and Muriel McCormack visit Charles Bickford in Dynamite.

Age (1933) and *Four Frightened People* (1934), neither of which was characteristic, the rest of his films, with the possible exception of *The Greatest Show on Earth* (1952) were all based on historical themes.

With the first of these historical based pictures, *Cleopatra,* in 1934, DeMille returned to the spectacle genre, a form which he never was to leave again.

Cleopatra is a sexual extravaganza in which DeMille reveled at his erotic best. Claudette Colbert in the title role and a variety of Paramount contractees appear in the briefest of gowns and togas in some remarkable sets. The Royal Barge, for example, is an incredible fabrication, from its banks of oars each surmounted with a ram's head to the pillowed dais on which Cleopatra seduces Marc Antony. At her signal, an inexhaustible supply of slave girls bursts out of every door to perform a series of exotic dances; a garlanded ox is led in, to be caressed by semi-naked girls, one of whom in the second before fade-out assumes a pose of sexual surrender before the animal; a nude group is whipped into submission by a huge slave; a net-full of girls, clad only in sea-weed, is dredged up to sprawl out wriggling

Lillian Roth to Kay Johnson: "You haven't the temperament to win your husband back; men like 'em wild." (Madam Satan, *1930*).

A touch of the feline for Madam Satan.

Kay Johnson and Reginald Denny in Madam Satan.

A deluxe shower in a marble-walled bathroom (Madam Satan). *L. to r.: DeMille, Roland Young. Reginald Denny, and Kay Johnson.*

In this spectacular episode from Madam Satan, *a ballet takes place aboard a dirigible that eventually crashes.*

Kay Johnson in Madam Satan.

Who is Paul Cavanaugh's gun aimed at?

The 1931 version of Squaw Man *featured DeWitt Jennings, Charles Bickford, and Warner Baxter.*

Lupe Velez and Warner Baxter in Squaw Man.

Now it's Warner Baxter's turn to ride.

Warner Baxter in Squaw Man.

C. B. talks with some oldtimers on the Squaw Man *set.*

The heroic Warner Baxter . . . the demure Lupe Velez (Squaw Man).

on the deck and offer seashells full of jewels. When Antony succumbs to her wiles, Cleopatra gestures to the slaves and, as veils rise around her bed and singing girls strew them with flower petals, the cadence drummer strikes up the rhythm that sets the oars moving, and the barge moves slowly out to sea.

DeMille and Henry Wilcoxon, the young Britisher he signed for Marc Antony, hit it off with the first handshake. Wilcoxon was athletic and handsome enough to provide a good counterpart to Claudette Colbert's Cleopatra. Eventually, their friendship led Wilcoxon from actor to associate producer with C. B. on several projects. What had really cemented their close relationship was a fight scene toward the end of production.

According to Wilcoxon: "It was the scene where Marc Antony stands off 16 of his own men in the midst of general combat with the Egyptians. Every few minutes, C. B. would stop the fight and shout, 'Get in there and fight like you mean it! You're not supposed

Claudette Colbert poses as a "temptress" in Sign of the Cross.

to be playing. You're trying to kill each other.'

"He finally lost his temper and stormed over to us to give a demonstration of what he wanted. He grabbed a spear and shield from one of the soldiers, cautioned me to defend myself, and yelled, 'This is the way I want you to fight.'

"DeMille rushed at me like he was going to cut me to pieces. All swords in his films were real, not rubber. I had a helluva time keeping him off, and after a few minutes my whole body was wet and I was trying to find a way to end it. I finally succeeded in sidestepping, and as he lunged I cut his spear in half, backed up and threw my weapon on the ground.

"Without a sign of fatigue, he turned to the men, 'If you don't want to fight like that you can leave the set!' And a lot of them did."

During the ensuing scene, Wilcoxon had one leg cut to the bone and the end of a little finger chopped off. When they ran the sequence in the projection room, C. B. whispered in the actor's ear,

Clarence Burton and Nat Pendleton discover the Sign of the Cross *(1932).*

Claudette Colbert takes a bath in ass's milk (Sign of the Cross).

Fredric March pleads Christianity's cause before Emperor Charles Laughton. Empress Claudette Colbert watches (Sign of the Cross).

Battle-ready March wants a last kiss from Claudette (Sign of the Cross).

Miss Colbert cajoles Charles Laughton as Ian Keith looks on (Sign of the Cross).

Elissa Landi and Fredric March, and Joyzelle Joyner in Sign of the Cross.

Love blooms between Roman Fredric March and Christian Elissa Landi (Sign of the Cross).

"It's almost as good as the fight we put on."

The most remarkable sequence in *Cleopatra,* however, is when Colbert as the Queen of the Nile realizes the end is near and thrusts an asp to her breast.

Filming this scene was held for the very last because Colbert loathed snakes, and when DeMille told her how it ended, she had refused to do it with a live snake. Insisting on realism, he had demanded that she do it or give up the part. She wavered and C. B. had told her that they would put off the discussion until it was time to shoot it.

The picture was in the can with the exception of the asp-suicide scene. The day of shooting, C. B. arrived on the set with a huge, but docile boa constrictor coiled about his neck and shoulder.

Behind his back he held a six-inch garden snake. As he advanced to Colbert, seated on her throne, she started shouting, "Oh, Mr. DeMille, don't come near me with that!" He continued and her protestations grew louder. When he was almost at her feet he said, "Well, how about this one?" and handed her the tiny snake, worm-

Ben Alexander does some entertaining in a nightclub (This Day and Age, *1933*).

Harry Green, Judith Allen, and Charles Bickford in This Day and Age.

Charles Bickford is a victim of Richard Cromwell and Eddie Nugent in This Day and Age.

Bickford gets ready for some action (This Day and Age).

Bickford comes upon a burglary in progress (This Day and Age).

like by comparison. She giggled in relief, "Oh, the poor little thing. It's scared to death."

Clutching the snake to her bosom, she fulfilled Cleopatra's destiny and created a scene that movie fans will never forget. While the camera pans backward down the huge darkened throne-hall, she glares wild-eyed dead into eternity.

In *Cleopatra,* and in all his historical pictures, C. B.'s approach to factual history, one subordinate remarked, "was liberal." Dates, sequences, geography, character, names were bent to his needs. Yet at the same time, he was an undeviating realist about details. Harnesses had to be exact, wagon wheels, pots, weapons, and costumes of museum accuracy.

"*The Crusades,*" DeMille explained, "is a good example of what I call telescoping history. Actually there were several Crusades extending over two centuries. It would be impossible to tell the story of them all in two hours of film. Audiences are not interested in dates, but in events and their significance. And they do not want to be educated, but entertained.

Had Claudette Colbert been present, she might have told William Gargan and Herbert Marshall not to fight over her. She wasn't, though, so they did (Four Frightened People).

The cobra is ready to strike as (l. to r.) Mary Boland, Herbert Marshall, William Gargan, and Claudette Colbert wait (Four Frightened People).

The Four Frightened People *face some of the jungle natives.*

William Gargan points an accusing finger (Four Frightened People).

More terror for Claudette Colbert and William Gargan (Four Frightened People).

"We chose the year 1187 as the focal point for our story, but did not hesitate to bring in elements from the other crusades. I submit that a person seeing this film can come away with a very good idea of what the crusades were all about without having been subjected to a day-by-day chronological presentation of actual fact."

"If you'll look back," one of his associates said, more in awe than in criticism, "you will note that C. B. has gone through the centuries like the Headless Horseman. Heaven only knows how many months and years he has misplaced."

Possibly because the motion picture industry is highly competitive, to say the least, DeMille was suspected by his peers at Paramount as flaunting the natural laws of occupancy. After all hadn't the father of the industry, D. W. Griffith, faded with the coming of sound? DeMille was watched closely for signs of approaching debility in the mid-thirties. When *The Crusades* suffered the unique experience of losing more than $700,000, Adolph Zukor, still head of Paramount, clapped his hands mournfully to his face and cried, "The king is dead!"

A set design of part of the famous Baths at Rome, which Cecil B. DeMille reconstructed for Cleopatra.

In this sumptuous scene from Cleopatra *(1934), Claudette Colbert entertains Henry Wilcoxon on her barge.*

Surrounded by her retinue, Miss Colbert prepares for her meeting with Marc Antony (Cleopatra).

C. B. always went first class.

In these two love scenes from Cleopatra, *Claudette Colbert was romanced in turn by Warren William (Caesar) and Henry Wilcoxon (Antony).*

One of the exotic costumes Claudette Colbert wore in Cleopatra.

Henry Wilcoxon as he appeared in Cleopatra.

Preparing for battle (The Crusades, *1935*).

Henry Wilcoxon in The Crusades.

Loretta Young in The Crusades: *in the camp of Ian Keith, a Moslem leader.*

Miss Young pledges her troth.

Henry Wilcoxon in The Crusades.

Wilcoxon and Loretta Young in The Crusades.

Henry Wilcoxon as King Richard the Lion-Hearted orders an assault on the Moslems (The Crusades) .

Katherine DeMille, Henry Wilcoxon, and Loretta Young face a tense moment (The Crusades).

DeMille himself was shaken by the reception accorded *The Crusades,* but he rallied stoutly the following year and, with something akin to vengeance, replaced the fallen heroes of the Crusades with Indians and presented *The Plainsman* (1937). With Gary Cooper as Wild Bill Hickok and Jean Arthur as Calamity Jane, this film began DeMille's series on American history, but lacked the impact of two later films, *The Buccaneer* (1938), with Fredric March in one of his best roles as Jean Lafitte, and *Union Pacific* (1939) with Barbara Stanwyck and Joel McCrea. *The Plainsman,* however, does have one unforgettable moment. As Cooper's body lies on the saloon floor after his murder, DeMille dissolves so that it seems to melt into the earth. Hickok has become part of the land and its mythology. This is an image of a genuine cinematic poet.

During production of *Plainsman,* DeMille demonstrated that he asked no more of his actors than he was willing to do himself. In a scene, Jean Arthur was required to flick a gun out of an actor's hand

Cooper and Arthur in The Plainsman, *1937.*

Gary Cooper, Anthony Quinn, and James Ellison in The Plainsman.

Jean Arthur and Porter Hall are shocked at Gary Cooper's death (The Plainsman).

Gary Cooper as Wild Bill Hickock in The Plainsman.

Jean Arthur and Gary Cooper (The Plainsman).

The Plainsman, *Gary Cooper gets the drop on two desperadoes . . .*

but here the Indians seem to have gotten the better of our hero.

Pirate protector of Franciska Gaal, diminutive Hungarian actress cast opposite Fredric March in The Buccaneer *(1938), is Akim Tamiroff (r.) who appears as Dominique You, the famous gunner of Napoleon who became pirate Jean Lafitte's chief lieutenant. March is seen as Lafitte.*

A lady walks the plank. Pirate Lafitte's mutineers force Franciska Gaal to walk the plank. The man in the officer's coat is Robert Barrat, leader of a mutiny against March (The Buccaneer).

American warships in Barataria Bay blast at the pirates, who have rowed out peacefully to meet them. An incident of the days when the Americans and British were fighting the War of 1812 (The Buccaneer).

Akim Tamiroff, Fredric March and Anthony Quinn (The Buccaneer).

The young man at the right is Jack Bickel of East Orange, N.J., brother of Fredric March, left. The Bickel boys are shown with C. B. DeMille on the set of The Buccaneer.

As a result of this screen test, pretty Franciska Gaal won the leading feminine role opposite Fredric March in DeMille's The Buccaneer. *DeMille is shown directing her.*

Barbara Stanwyck and Robert Preston were the stars of Union Pacific *(1939).*

with a 12-foot whip, something the actor did not relish in view of Miss Arthur's inexperience. DeMille quickly offered his own arm as a practice target and took a fairly severe lashing before the actress' aim improved to the point where the actor was willing to risk it.

C. B. found Gary Cooper to be an "affable, modest American gentleman and an accomplished actor." He so much enjoyed working with him that he gave him the lead in three other films: *North West Mounted Police* (1940), *The Story of Dr. Wassell* (1944) and *The Unconquered* (1947).

In *North West Mounted Police,* DeMille dyed Paulette Goddard's face nut brown for her role as an Indian girl who seduces Robert Preston in a spiritedly staged sequence in C. B.'s most punchy man-

Joel McCrea (l.) joins Robert Preston and Barbara Stanwyck as they attempt to stand off enemies of the railroad (Union Pacific).

The Union Pacific *runs into some Indian trouble.*

Robert Preston (l.) and Brian Donlevy have their differences in Union Pacific.

Typical western, typical DeMille, crowd scene for Union Pacific.

Laying the historic rails (Union Pacific) .

Joel McCrea slugs it out with rebellious worker (Union Pacific).

Laying of the golden spike (Union Pacific).

The railroads are united (Union Pacific).

Preston Foster is the mountie confronting Gary Cooper in this scene from North West Mounted Police, *1940.*

Gary Cooper pauses to relax in North West Mounted Police.

Madeleine Carroll and Gary Cooper in North West Mounted Police.

Akim Tamiroff, Gary Cooper, and Lynne Overman in North West Mounted Police.

The Mounties get their man, George Bancroft.

Preston Foster and Gary Cooper have an animated discussion in North West Mounted Police.

C. B. shows Paulette Goddard and Robert Preston the proper way to do a scene of North West Mounted Police. *The muscular Indian is Dick Klein, a physical education instructor.*

Fighting glamor girl Paulette Goddard takes a nip out of Lynne Overman's knee (North West Mounted Police).

Because C. B. was too busy filming Reap the Wild Wind, *manager Sid Grauman of Grauman's Chinese Theater brought a block of wet cement to the director. Martha O'Driscoll looks on (1942).*

ner. Bosley Crowther, dean of the New York movie critics, wrote of the film, "Barely did we anticipate something so colossal."

Also in this period DeMille directed *Reap the Wild Wind* (1942). His sixtieth birthday came during the shooting of this exciting sea-adventure with John Wayne, Ray Milland and Paulette Goddard. Besides giving momentum to Susan Hayward's budding career, this color costume adventure's chief attraction was a giant artificial octopus which was one of the screen's most convincing studio-made creatures.

"For the first time in my life," DeMille blurted happily, "I'm being helped to make a picture instead of being dared to make one." And since he was too busy on the set to go to Hollywood Boulevard, Sid Grauman, owner of the Grauman's Chinese Theatre, brought a block of wet cement to the studio to receive C. B.'s hand and footprints, bestowing on DeMille Hollywood's own brand of immortality.

C. B. enjoys a day off sailing his yacht.

DeMille, who had just turned 60 at the time, shows a stunt man how to swing down the length of a ship during the shooting of Reap the Wild Wind.

In this scene the stuntman had to smash through the wheel (the spoke had been fixed to break easily).

Susan Hayward, Ray Milland, and Paulette Goddard in Reap the Wild Wind.

Blood vs. love: Ray Milland (r.) plays upon Robert Preston's love for Susan Hayward to get him to turn State's evidence against his own brother, Raymond Massey (l.) in this scene from Reap the Wild Wind. *Massey, in the role of the "brains" of a ring of piratical ship wreckers who swarm the Florida Keys, is also Milland's opposing counsel in court.*

Contempt of court: Infuriated when he learns that his own brother, Raymond Massey, may have caused the death of the girl he loves, Robert Preston vaults over a chair to get at Massey's throat (Reap the Wild Wind).

Paulette Goddard goes to Charleston to intercede for John Wayne. Ray Milland, attorney for the firm and Wayne's rival, falls for her wiles, but turns her over his knee and spanks her when he discovers in the midst of a grand ball that she has been merely using him to promote Wayne's career (Reap the Wild Wind).

An underwater scene from Reap the Wild Wind.

Amused John Wayne looks on as Paulette Goddard confronts Raymond Massey (Reap the Wild Wind).

John Wayne and Paulette Goddard take cover (Reap the Wild Wind).

Wayne had planned an elopement here, but Paulette Goddard has to intercede for Ray Milland (Reap the Wild Wind).

Paulette Goddard flirts with Milland (Reap the Wild Wind).

DeMille is perched high on a camera boom 45 feet above the ground, as he directs a scene for The Story of Dr. Wassell. *Note that the pioneer movie-king has by now abandoned the old-fashioned megaphone for a hand microphone and a P.A. system (1944).*

Gary Cooper receives a medal (Dr. Wassell).

Dennis O'Keefe and Carol Thurston in Dr. Wassell.

Gary Cooper and Signe Hasso are wartime doctor-and-nurse team (Dr. Wassell).

Laraine Day listens to radio for rescue signal (Dr. Wassell).

Helmeted Gary Cooper looks properly heroic in Dr. Wassell.

Gary Cooper watches as the Japanese blow up a bridge in Java (Dr. Wassell).

Cooper directs a rescue scene (Dr. Wassell).

Paulette Goddard as Abigail Hale and Gary Cooper as Captain Christopher Holden, in DeMille's Unconquered *(1947).*

Gary Cooper and Paulette Goddard find themselves in trouble in Unconquered.

Gary Cooper and Paulette Goddard fend off trouble (Unconquered).

Paulette Goddard about to suffer at the hands of the Indian . . . or is she?

Paulette in trouble again (Unconquered).

Jeanie MacPherson, the scenarist on many of DeMille's pictures.

Amateur deep-sea adventurer DeMille took to a diving suit now and again.

Mr. DeMille and Paramount Studio starlet in 1936 Cord.

Katherine DeMille in close-up.

The arena scene from The Sign of the Cross.

C. Aubrey Smith is slain with arrows in The Crusades.

DeMille directs scene from This Day and Age *(1933.)*

DeMille studies scene sketches for The Sign of the Cross, *1932.*

Judith Allan, Richard Cromwell, Eddie Nugent, player and DeMille pose for a publicity shot on the set of This Day and Age, *1933.*

An extremely rare shot of DeMille directing Claudette Colbert in Cleopatra, *1934.*

Madeleine Carroll and Gary Cooper in North West Mounted Police, *1940.*

DeMille, in preparing The Buccaneer *for Fredric March, miniature costume models for authenticity, 1937.*

6

"Put millions of dollars into a Sunday school story?"

For over a decade, DeMille had been thinking on and off about one of the greatest love stories in the world, that of Samson and Delilah. But when he presented the idea to the new heads of Paramount, they expressed serious misgivings: "Put millions of dollars into a Sunday school story?" C. B. finally convinced them by reducing the story elements to "boy meets girl—and what a boy, and what a girl!"

"I'm sometimes accused of gingering up the Bible with lavish infusions of sex and violence," he explained then, "but I wish that my accusers would read their Bibles more closely, for in those pages are more violence and sex than I could ever portray on the screen."

Casting the two principals began with DeMille hiring researchers to collect as many pictures of paintings of Samson and Delilah by the old masters, like Rembrandt and others, as were available. Having a large religious library and a reputation as a Hollywood Biblical scholar (he read from the Bible every day), he was anxious to portray the characters as authentically as possible. Unable to come up with a painting of Delilah that he especially favored, he hired an artist to render one that was more to his liking. This new painting served as the model in the ensuing national talent search for the female lead.

Nothing came of the search, either for Delilah or Samson, except a whale of a lot of publicity. He finally decided on Hedy Lamarr and Victor Mature in the roles because "they embody in the public mind the essence of maleness and femininity."

He then set his researchers to documenting how people dressed, ate and generally behaved in those days. DeMille frequently pointed

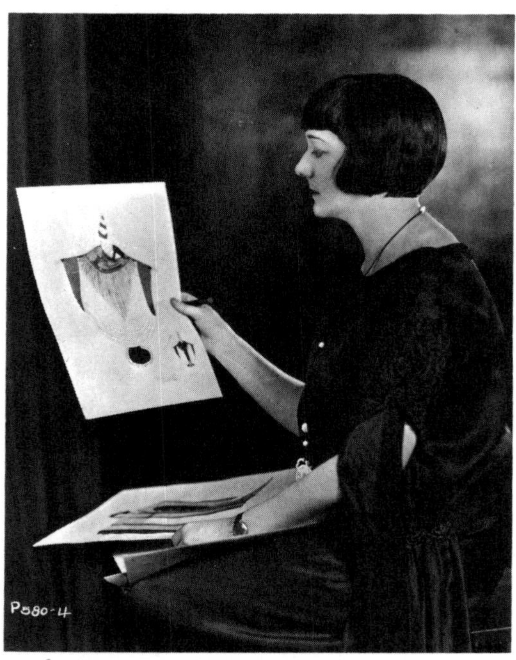

This is the way costumes for Cecil B. DeMille productions were designed. Claire West, shown here, painted them on cardboard and submitted them to Mr. DeMille before the actual making of the costumes began. She made frequent trips to Europe to keep ahead of the style trends both in this country and abroad.

out to his detractors that he spent in excess of $100,000 on research for every picture he ever made with a historical background. How and if something actually happened was of paramount importance.

"Do you suppose Samson really killed all those Philistines with the jawbone of an ass?" he mused one day in his office. He quickly rang up the prop man, Joe Thompson, obviously a man who was not easily stumped for he brought DeMille the jawbone of an ass as requested. The director fondled it in his hand. He slashed at imaginary Philistines rushing in through the office door until they were piled high in front of his massive desk.

Then he looked at every piece of art he could find that depicted the scene. Invariably, only half a jawbone was shown in Samson's hand. "Something funny here," he grumbled impatiently.

Art somehow had erred. It was apparently impossible to smash down through a Philistine helmet with only half a jawbone. On

Victor Mature pulls down idol in Samson and Delilah, *1949.*

Hedy La Marr as Delilah and blinded Victor Mature as Samson (Samson and Delilah).

Victor Mature in Samson and Delilah.

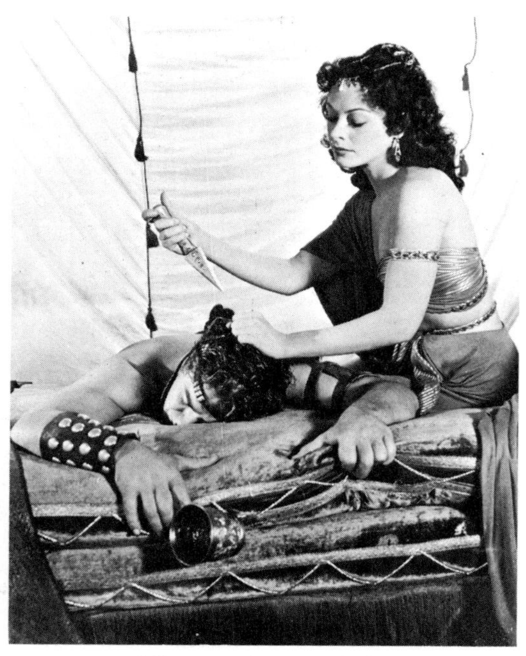

Samson gets world's most famous haircut from Delilah.

Victor Mature in Samson and Delilah.

George Sanders cast as a staunch Philistine ruler (Samson and Delilah).

Hedy La Marr and Victor Mature enjoy an affectionate outdoor bath (Samson and Delilah).

Hedy La Marr and Victor Mature in Samson and Delilah.

Philistine warrior tries to capture Victor Mature (Samson) in Samson and Delilah.

the other hand, a full jawbone was quite a lethal weapon, with a natural grip in the region of the chin. So Samson used a *full* jawbone in the picture.

At the same time that DeMille would dogmatically spend a fortune to learn the exact letters and figures carved on an ancient temple wall, he would also in every film work in some reference to his family background, of which he was exceedingly proud. He often pointed out that his forebears had come from Holland to what is now Manhattan some 300 years ago in a ship called *The Gilded Beaver.* In *The Unconquered,* which was laid in pre-Revolutionary America, DeMille named a frontier drinking establishment The Gilded Beaver. DeMille's middle name was Blount. To the surprise of no one except historians, a waterfront site in *The Unconquered* showed up as Blount's Landing.

A more obvious manifestation of DeMille's propensity for family references in his motion pictures was the launching of the screen career of his adopted daughter Katherine DeMille with *Madam Satan* in 1930. She appeared in such other films as *The Crusades* and *The Unconquered.* She later married Anthony Quinn, who began his

Hedy La Marr wears fabled peacock costume for Samson and Delilah. *DeMille himself collected each feather one by one on his ranch.*

association with C. B. playing a minor part in *The Plainsman,* supporting roles in *The Buccaneer* and *Union Pacific,* and eventually directed a second version of *The Buccaneer* under DeMille's indirect supervision in 1959.

In *Samson and Delilah,* although there was no one named Blount or DeMille in Biblical times, C. B. managed a family reference by naming one of the picture's minor characters Gammad, after a favorite uncle.

Cecil B. DeMille was undoubtedly the best known director in the world, decorated by many governments and blessed by the Pope, and finally he was singled out by the Industry that he had fathered from its early days to receive its highest recognition, the Academy Award, for his next film, *The Greatest Show on Earth.* Strangely, he received only three Oscars in his 45-year career. First, in 1950 as a general recognition of "thirty-seven years of brilliant showmanship," given as a sop to Hollywood's conscience; and secondly, for *Greatest Show,* his 69th and the weakest of his last great films, again as an apology that perhaps he had been neglected. Then, as if to verify what had merely been suggested by his second Oscar, the

DeMille, pictured here with Henry Wilcoxon, poses with Academy Award for The Greatest Show on Earth *(1952) and the Thalberg Award.*

One of the disaster scenes from DeMille's The Greatest Show on Earth.

Cornel Wilde, Betty Hutton, and Gloria Grahame in train wreck scene from **The Greatest Show on Earth.**

Betty Hutton shows love for Cornel Wilde, her high-wire rival (The Greatest Show on Earth).

James Stewart and Charlton Heston aid Cornel Wilde, who has fallen from a high wire (The Greatest Show on Earth).

Actress Gloria Grahame with Lyle Bettger (The Greatest Show on Earth).

Charlton Heston, Lyle Bettger and James Stewart in The Greatest Show on Earth.

Betty Hutton and James Stewart in The Greatest Show on Earth.

DeMille used the cast of the Ringling Brothers' Circus for The Greatest Show on Earth. *Here several of the performers do one of their famous routines.*

Betty Hutton and Charlton Heston in The Greatest Show on Earth.

Lovely Dorothy Lamour in The Greatest Show on Earth.

Academy of Motion Picture Arts and Sciences voted him the Irving Thalberg Award, which is bestowed on rare occasions to a film-maker for outstanding years of producing and directing.

Lesser directors have received the Academy Award several times. This slight did not present the only irony.

The critics seemed always to crucify DeMille for his screen efforts. "Nobody likes Mr. DeMille's pictures except the public," one of his staff said. And comedian Bob Hope once quipped, "Cecil B. DeMille is indeed Mr. Motion Picture. His films have brought something new to the theatres. They call them customers."

However, DeMille rarely turned down an opportunity to play himself on film, and he made a score of cameo appearances in Paramount pictures of the thirties and forties. He also filmed special prologues for his motion pictures, in which he personally addressed the audience before his pictures unwound, and preview trailers in which he told moviegoers why they should see his current release. His appearance as himself in *Sunset Boulevard* remains his best performance before the cameras.

DeMille plays himself opposite Gloria Swanson in Sunset Boulevard, *1950.*

In his first 37 years in Hollywood, DeMille produced 68 films, most of them triumphant. A millionaire several times over, he typified the system by which people become millionaires: he spent dollars and saved pennies.

For his first 68 pictures, he spent a total of nearly $30 million, yet as the story goes, he was known to buy an apple in Albuquerque and carry the core to New York and back across the country again to use as a sweetener in a tobacco container at home. At his ranch, Paradise, he bought government surplus potatoes at 5¢ a hundredweight for the deer with which he'd made friends. Shrewdly, he resold the sacks the potatoes came in for 7¢ apiece. Thus, he not only received the potatoes free, but turned a 2-penny profit with each sack.

On the other hand, he willingly paid Ringling Brothers $250,000 for the right to use the circus's name and equipment in *Greatest Show on Earth.* His previous picture, *Samson and Delilah,* budgeted at $2.5 million, included such strenuous expenditures as $392,547 for the cast, $124,127 for the wardrobe, $119,594 for the construction of the sets, and $64,159 for the sound recording.

Charlton Heston and Yul Brynner in The Ten Commandments, *1957.*

The river flows the color of blood in this dramatic scene. Henry Wilcoxon, Yul Brynner, Charlton Heston, and John Carradine in The Ten Commandments.

The endless cavalcade of the Biblical Exodus through the Avenue of Sphinxes at the gates of the city of Per-Rameses, as seen in DeMille's The Ten Commandments.

Julia Faye, John Carradine, John Derek, Charlton Heston in The Ten Commandments.

In the matter of budgets, DeMille was looked upon as something of a genius, making things come out even, though he could not explain how he did it. His system of measuring the length of a picture, for budgetary purposes, was to count the words of dialogue in the script. He counted a foot of film for every word. Despite the fact that there are fast talkers, slow talkers, rapid scenes and sluggish scenes, it seemed to work. In *Reap the Wild Wind,* there was a reel and a half with no dialogue whatever, yet the count came out right. DeMille had no idea why.

The most impressive thing about his pictures was that the $30 million invested had to that date, 1950, returned a gross of $562 million.

Samson and Delilah, which was mercilessly ripped by critics, balancing the raves precariously, as it turned out, was the direct precursor of such incredibly costly and successful epics as *Quo Vadis* (1951), *The Robe* (1953), and even DeMille's own *The Ten Commandments* (1956), which in turn led to others like *Ben Hur* (1959) and *The King of Kings* (1961).

For more than twenty years, and increasingly after the release of *Samson and Delilah,* the customers that DeMille had brought into the theatres had been writing to him from all over the world, urging him to remake *The Ten Commandments.* "The world needs a reminder," the letters repeated, "of the Law of God."

But as always the idea had to be sold to Paramount executives. It had a strong champion in Hollywood, Frank Freeman, and one in New York, Adolph Zukor. Others, mildly stated, were less enthusiastic about another Biblical picture despite the profits realized by *Samson and Delilah.*

Finally, it was settled and DeMille was allowed to go ahead with plans. And for the first time in his career, there was never a question about the budget, which was originally penciled in at about $8 million but had scaled beyond $13 million before C. B. finished.

The script was three years in the writing. Meanwhile, Edith Head and her staff were designing costumes, John Fulton was preparing to part the Red Sea again, Leroy Prinz was studying Egyptian wall-paintings to insure authenticity for the sets.

More painstakingly than ever before, DeMille assembled a magnificent cast: Yul Brynner, Edward G. Robinson, Anne Baxter, Yvonne DeCarlo, Henry Wilcoxon (who also functioned as associate producer), John Derek, Vincent Price, Debra Paget, Judith Anderson and H. B. Warner. And headlining the list was Charlton Heston

The Red Sea came crashing in on the Egyptians in the second version of The Ten Commandments.

Charlton Heston defies Anne Baxter, who seeks his love, in this scene from The Ten Commandments.

Yvonne DeCarlo played Sephora, the wife of Moses, in The Ten Commandments.

Charlton Heston (c.), Vincent Price (l.), and John Derek (r.) wait for a decision.

Charlton Heston appears before the King (Yul Brynner) and the Queen (Anne Baxter) to plead for the freeing of the Jews (The Ten Commandments).

as Moses. "There had never been any doubt in my mind about who should play Moses," said C. B. "And my choice was strikingly affirmed when I had a sketch made of Chuck in a white beard and compared it to Michaelangelo's famous statue. The resemblance was amazing.

"But it wasn't merely an external resemblance. Charlton Heston brought to the role a rapidly maturing skill as an actor and an earnest understanding of the human and the spiritual quality of Moses. He had done the lead for me in *The Greatest Show* and had grown considerably since that film."

C. B. arranged for all the outdoor scenes to be filmed in Egypt, using the Valley of the Kings and Queen Hatsheput's tomb as the background and some 7,000 of the King's cavalry as extras. "Are you negotiating through the State Department," he was asked. "Oh no," he replied airily, "I don't bother with them. I deal directly with the rulers of the country."

When the 74-year-old C. B. announced that he was going to Egypt to supervise shooting, it was taken by some as a publicity stunt, thinking that the producer-director would stay a couple of days and

The Exodus begins.

return. They should have known better than to underestimate him. He stayed for the entire two months the location filming required.

This film was very close to him and he wanted every foot to be perfect. His drive for perfection had moved him to spend the entire summer of 1949 with the traveling Ringling Brothers Circus to learn that business from the inside out for *The Greatest Show on Earth.*

In Egypt, his cast of 20,000 all had to be costumed and assembled at eight different locations. Engineers built probably the largest movie set in history to simulate the gates of Biblical Per-Rameses, and a 16-sphinx avenue, which drew more tourists than Giza's single sphinx. Technicians rounded up hundreds of horses, innumerable sheep, camels, asses, water buffalo and geese.

On the location site, he worked 12 hours a day under the desert sun, racing from one camera position to another in an open Jeep. He clambered up steep slopes to gain properly epic vantage points. He even rode camel-back to the top of Mount Sinai to shoot the climactic scene in which Moses receives the Word of God. Also by camel, he traveled to the base camp on the Plains of Elias.

During a scene in which charioteers burst through the gates of Per-Rameses in pursuit of the Jews, DeMille moved his cameras to the top of the gates. Then he climbed 111 feet on a rickety ladder so he could supervise the shot. It was nearly his final exertion. He was suddenly stricken by an excruciating pain in his chest before he reached the top.

Somehow he managed to hang on and drag himself up to the top. Brushing off cameramen who were alarmed at his affliction, he finished the shot and then climbed back down unassisted. The company doctor, arriving immediately upon the scene, diagnosed it as a massive heart attack. It was not his first.

An oxygen tent, anticoagulants and complete bed rest was prescribed, to which DeMille scoffed, "I would rather be a dead director on the set, than a live director in an oxygen tent. What chance do I have if I carry on?" *Very poor,* he was told, but bull-headedly, he reported to work early the following morning, his worry-racked doctor at his side. He bumped wildly over the location in his Jeep.

An early scene sketch for the parting of the Red Sea in The Ten Commandments.

Edward G. Robinson harangues crowd in front of the Golden Calf (The Ten Commandments).

The adoration of the Golden Calf. Debra Paget is shown in chains.

Charlton Heston, as Moses, shows the tablets containing The Ten Commandments to his followers.

He darted indignantly up a hill to remove a modern halter from one of his Biblical donkeys.

DeMille maintained this incredible pace for another three weeks until location shooting was finished, and then ordered the entire operation back to Hollywood where filming was resumed.

Although DeMille drove himself far harder than he did anyone else, he was a very demanding man to work for, an exacting and merciless film maker. He readily conceded that he could be, and frequently was, a stern taskmaster. "I have been called a tyrant, a despot and a martinet," he once said. "But sometimes I lose my temper when I see somebody playing checkers on a set that costs $40,000 a day when he should be paying attention to his job. It's the same with alibis. I don't have enough time on this earth to listen to alibis."

Like any director, he was under terrific pressure. Already behind him when he began production on *Ten Commandments* were the years of preparation and ahead of him laid the unknown. At times like that he enjoyed thinking of himself as a general going into battle.

Cecil B. DeMille chats with Hedda Hopper and Clair McDowell, his leading lady in a stage production in 1902 in New York, on the set of his 66th screen production, Reap the Wild Wind, *1942.*

Upon the return of the *Ten Commandments* production crew to Paramount, it dominated the entire studio lot, occupying twelve of the eighteen sound stages. To film the seven-minute sequence where the Red Sea parts to allow the Children of Israel to pass and then falls on the Egyptians, more space was needed and found by breaking down the fences and spreading out in the adjoining RKO lot. A 300,000-gallon tank was built and filled with water to double for the Red Sea, the parting of which benefited greatly from the improved techniques since the 1923 version, winning the Special Effects Oscar that year.

As production progressed, invariably, DeMille got less and less sleep. He believed thoroughly in inspiration as a sudden, blinding flash of light, and he wanted always to be ready when it struck. This naturally required vigilance. Likewise, harnessing the inspiration, after it struck, to a camera could be a demanding business.

Gary Cooper in the Gilded Beaver Inn in The Unconquered, *1947.*

Billy Wilder directs Gloria Swanson and Cecil B. DeMille in a scene from Sunset Boulevard, *1950.*

Charlton Heston and Yul Brynner in The Ten Commandments.

When he returned home after a day's shooting, he was very nearly exhausted. Mrs. DeMille waited up for him no matter what the hour, and sat with him while he had dinner (which was ready at all times because the time of his arrival home was uncertain). If he wanted to talk, they talked, sometimes to three or four in the morning, after which he would sleep four hours and rise refreshed for the new day. If he didn't feel like talking, they didn't, and he would spend the rest of the night in a state of suspended alert. A pad and pencil were always within easy reach in case inspiration came.

When involved in his work, C. B. unintentionally overlooked breaks, lunches and quitting times. While directing a large number of extras for a crowd scene in the first *Ten Commandments,* he noticed one young lady whispering to another after he had called for silence. "Young lady," he thundered, "if what you have to say is more important than what I have to say, come up here and tell everyone."

She shook her head, but he insisted. Thinking that she was about to be fired, she came forward defiantly. "I said, 'I wonder when that bald-headed old sonuvabitch is going to call lunch.' "

"Lunch!" commanded C. B. with a reluctantly amused smile.

Despite the same title, DeMille's second version of *The Ten Commandments* hardly resembled his 1923 effort. The first version, which cost $1.4 million, was a prelude to a modern morality movie. The second production, which cost $13.5 million (the costliest film ever made until *Cleopatra* with Liz Taylor was produced in 1963), cleaves to the Book of Exodus, filling its gaps from the writings of ancient historians and from present-day archaeological deduction.

Although a film of reverent and gargantuan significance, *The Ten Commandments,* which proved to be DeMille's greatest achievement and his final motion picture, went undecorated by the Academy Awards, save for the Oscar for Special Effects. For a second time in his legendary life, he was deeply hurt.

His consolation was that movie goers the world over have acclaimed C. B.'s last production as the third best ever made. To date it has grossed over $40 million in the United States alone, trailing behind only *Gone With the Wind* and *The Sound of Music.*

After finishing the pre-production work on *The Buccaneer* (1958), which was being produced by his close associate Henry Wilcoxon, Cecil B. DeMille began work on the life story of Lord Baden-Powell, the founder of the Boy Scouts, for his next project.

7

"If the Old Man ever stops, he'll fall flat on his face."

Cecil B. DeMille fought to the end to preserve his place and power in the motion picture industry. The idea of stopping work, of retiring or even resting, was out of the question, even after two heart attacks. Every day he dressed and went to the office until he literally couldn't walk any more.

"If the Old Man ever stops," one of his employees remarked, "he'll fall flat on his face. He's cursed with momentum."

He remained alert and vigorous and expressed his congenital impatience when he was presented with a medical ultimatum: total bed rest or imminent death. Like a child, he seemed astonished at the seriousness of his condition. And for once he became obedient.

The morning of January 23, 1959, his bed was found empty. The distraught family went frantically searching. They discovered him sitting beside his wife, Constance, who, too ill to speak, possibly was not even aware of his presence. He was quietly holding her hand and seemed to be waiting.

Without a word, he went back to bed, where, with his Bible by his side, he died in his sleep a few hours later. *Time* Magazine editorialized: "Hollywood will never be its old colossal self again."

Cecil B. DeMille had been largely instrumental in building a world industry and founding a city; he had taken crucial steps in the shaping of a new art, and was more widely known to his contemporaries than any other director in history. And he was a religious propagandist with an appeal which, although criticized as being superficial, was possibly the most popular in terms of numbers of people reached.

When Cecil B. DeMille first came to Los Angeles to open the Mason Opera House with E. H. Southern, he played the role of one of the vagabonds in If I Were King. *He also played as a leading man for Belasco in* Lord Chumley.

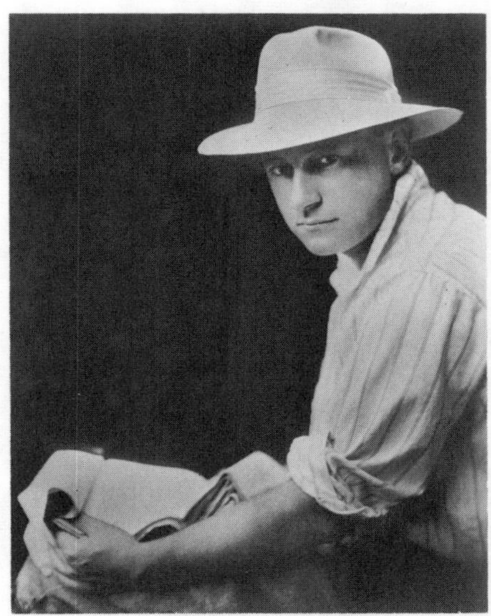

Cecil B. DeMille as the young actor.

DeMille, aviation pioneer, founded and operated Mercury Aviation Company, one of the first commercial air passenger services in the U.S. in 1919.

Aviation Trail Blazer. DeMille was the first member of the film colony to become an airplane pilot. His aviation company, Mercury Aviation, flew six planes on regular schedule between San Francisco, Los Angeles, and San Diego. With this company he inaugurated the regular flying of passengers and mail on schedule.

New and Old. DeMille poses with a new (in the 30s) camera and the one with which he filmed all his silent productions. The latter has his name stenciled on the side and has been exhibited in many museums.

"He could be the hardest and most terrifying man I ever met," Agnes DeMille later confided, "yet he sat beside many a deathbed because in the last moments it was his voice that was needed for comfort, his strength and his faith. People called to him when they were dying. This is a fact and it is unanswerable."

And it is interesting to know that a great sense of formality permeated all his relations. His sons- and daughters-in-law called him "Mister DeMille" to the day he died, never on any occasion "Father." And his staff would always address him as "Mister" or "Boss." He commanded their unyielding devotion and respect.

What he managed to instill in his staff and crews was that any picture they were working on was not only the only work of art currently being realized, but that it somehow had much to do with the continued well-being of the human race. On the set he commanded absolute power and as long as he stood by the camera, everyone's career was at stake. He could terminate careers, or make an

DeMille took off his coat, rolled up his sleeves, and went to work when he rehearsed the Lux Radio Theater, which was broadcast every Monday night over the CBS network from Hollywood.

unknown famous within an hour; his power within the industry was limitless.

The secret of his strength lies in his own words: "To transfer the Bible to the screen you cannot cheat; you have to *believe!*" And above all he believed in a prompt and attentive God, who always came through in the nick of time, exactly on schedule. C. B. chose episodes and characters that proved his doctrine, and disregarded whatever didn't. He always smashed through what was uncomfortable to what he wished to believe, to what he in effect succeeded in believing—that *right always triumphed.* "DeMille," in the words of another moviemaker, who paid tribute to him, "proved that God is big box office." When *The Ten Commandments* was in preparation in 1955, a press agent wanted to advertise the picture as: "You've read the best-selling book. Now see the movie!"

Never deviating from his early instruction, DeMille was elaborately fastidious on moral issues in his films, all the while playing on every erotic and sadistic instinct. Realizing that religion and sex were an explosive combination, he heightened the torture of naked women with the singing of hymns.

Frank Calvin (r.), scion of famous railroading family and son of the late E. E. Calvin, former president of both the Union Pacific and Southern Pacific railroads, is applying his knowledge of the railroads to the movies. He was engaged by DeMille to do research for a film of the first transcontinental railway, Union Pacific.

Elsie Janis in Hollywood. The famous stage comedienne, known to every American doughboy in France during World War I, visits DeMille on The North West Mounted Police *set.*

That stuff in the wheelbarrow may look like a child's toys, but it's really some very important material—a truck model filled with miniature figures DeMille used in planning a scene from The Story of Dr. Wassell.

Wild life in Hollywood. This study of DeMille and a deer named "Fearless Fosdick" was made at his Paradise Ranch by Yul Brynner.

DeMille and four scenes from his most famous films: (top l. to r.) The King of Kings, Cleopatra; *(bottom l. to r.)* The Ten Commandments, The Greatest Show on Earth.

Griffith was the first to show that films could depict sex and violence if virtue triumphed at the end. And DeMille always closed his pictures with the hymn rather than the orgy, and if the route to the divine was full of sensuous detours, the final victory was all the more meaningful.

Almost contradictorily, C. B. considered the writing of D. H. Lawrence and Ernest Hemingway salacious, and even though he often bordered on obscenity in his work, he was always somewhat prudish in his treatment of women.

DeMille's struggle for truth and justice was not limited to his motion pictures, but a fight he carried on daily in his private life.

Cecil B. DeMille and seven-passenger custom-built Cunningham Eight painted a Nile green with a thin gold stripe and cream wheels.

The most public example of this came in 1944 when, after having produced the Lux Radio Theatre of the Air Force at a salary of $98,200 a year, he received a letter from the Los Angeles local of the American Federation of Radio Artists. The letter notified DeMille that he was being assessed $1 to help the union finance a campaign in opposition to a proposed state amendment labeled Proposition 12 which called for the *open shop* in California.

DeMille personally supported Proposition 12, and therefore refused to pay $1 to support an opposing viewpoint through the union. Although the union bent over backwards trying to compromise with him, even extending the deadline date for payment, C. B. refused to sacrifice his beliefs. He gave up his show, and the salary that went with it, rather than pay the assessment that he considered illegal. He quoted Thomas Jefferson in support of his stand: "To compel a man to furnish contributions of money for the propagation of opinions which he disbelieves is sinful and tyrannical."

When the courts ruled against him, he founded the DeMille

Anne Bauchens was his top film cutter who examined the thousands of feet of film made for a DeMille production.

DeMille believes in having everything on paper.

Anna Christie—*Marjorie Rambeau, George Marion, Joan Crawford, and DeMille. A Lux Theatre Radio Production of 1938.*

Then Vice President Richard Nixon presents the Freedoms Foundation Award to C. B. DeMille in February 1953. At left is Kenneth Wells, president of the Foundation, and the Rev. Fulton J. Sheen, Catholic Bishop, receiving an award for his TV program, "Life is Worth Living." DeMille was honored for his public address, "Silent Voices."

1954. Mr. and Mrs. Cecil B. DeMille in a rare public appearance.

Foundation for Political Freedom which has continued to fight for what he called "the right to work."

The Lux Show had an estimated thirty million listeners. According to associates, DeMille was never happier or easier to get along with. Eventually he became as proud of the show as if he were producing a spectacle a week. But his integrity was more important.

And just as he believed in himself, he had faith in his work and in motion pictures. When other producers ran scared and ceased production because of the onslaught of television, which brought about the black decade in Hollywood, he stood firm.

"You're not going to wipe out theatres with home television or anything else," DeMille asserted. "*The Ten Commandments* on a 46-foot screen is a completely different thing from the same film on a 24-inch screen. You put Rosa Bonheur's *The Horse Fair* on a postage stamp and you'll not be able to see even the horses.

While Henry Wilcoxon watches from the background, DeMille shows an extra how to carry a shoulder balance on location in Egypt for "The Ten Commandments," 1956.

"And there still is no way that television can underwrite productions of the size we're dealing with now. A picture like *The Ten Commandments* doesn't come with Lipton's Tea."

During the course of his screen career DeMille's energy occasionally propelled him outside the realm of motion pictures. One of his most notable excursions took him into aviation, when he founded what was probably the first air line in the United States to carry passengers on regular scheduled flights.

In 1917 he had tried to get into the war but was rejected because of age—unless, they told him, he could fly, in which case he could join the Army Air Corps. DeMille was stumped. He couldn't learn to fly because he couldn't find a plane. Then one day he read in the newspapers where a man had killed himself in a Jenny in Canada.

Her Majesty Queen Elizabeth II chats with Cecil B. DeMille. At right, Lord Rank, and at left, Lady French and Sir Henry French. 1957.

DeMille, Yul Brynner and Henry Wilcoxon examine some research items in the preparation of The Buccaneer, *1959.*

Thirty-two film stars whose careers were boosted by Producer Cecil B. DeMille join him for an historic photo at the Beverly Hilton where he was presented the Screen Producers Guild Milestone Award for historic contribution to the motion picture. Left to right, front row: Jesse L. Lasky, Virginia Grey, Loretta Young, Julia Faye, Walter Brennan, Jane Darwell, Winifred Kingston, DeMille, Barbara Stanwyck, Reginald Denny, Kathlyn Williams, Claudette Colbert, Raymond Hatton, Susan Hayward, Katherine DeMille Quinn, Beulah Bondi, Eddie Quillan. Back row: Rod LaRoque, Fredric March, Ben Alexander, Richard Cromwell, Ricardo Cortez, Paul Kelly, Yul Brynner, Laraine Day, Charlton Heston, William Boyd, Lon Chaney, Jr., Gary Cooper, Ward Bond, Anthony Quinn, Henry Wilcoxon, James Stewart. Lasky was DeMille's first producer back in 1913, and all the others appeared in DeMille movies during the intervening years.

The director promptly telephoned the man's widow, bought the wrecked plane for $5,000, and had it expressed to Hollywood.

He went right to work learning to fly, but by the time he had become proficient enough to join the service, the war was over. Not to waste all that effort, he struck upon the idea of starting an air line. The Mercury Aviation Company was formed in 1919 with DeMille as president, and eventually it had a dozen planes, including two German Junkers, all metal mono-planes, which Eddie Rickenbacker flew out to California for the new company. The regular schedule connected Los Angeles, San Diego and San Francisco, and the line also operated non-scheduled flights all the way to Chicago and New York, in a leapfrog fashion of course.

Mercury Aviation was finally disbanded in 1921, partly because it had lost some $300,000 and partly because DeMille felt that he could not operate in two growing industries at once. In addition, Zukor habitually went out to the field and stood on the ground watching nervously. He was completely unnerved by the possibility that DeMille might come crashing down in the middle of a picture.

Reluctantly, DeMille abandoned his air line with: "The motion picture industry is growing tremendously, but in five years, aviation will be bigger than motion pictures ever could." Eventually, he gave up flying, even as a hobby.

DeMille also pioneered, as an officer of a Los Angeles bank and later of the Bank of America which absorbed it, in persuading banks to loan money and invest in motion pictures, a major factor in the early development of the industry.

On his last day at the studio, twelve days before he died, DeMille remarked as he was leaving to go home, "We have a lot of work to do in the next three years." He had in mind to complete two more pictures before retiring, *On My Honor,* the Lord Baden-Powell story, and one he planned as his last and greatest, which he referred to as "Project X," a project that died with him.

Except for a few indications given to his closest co-workers, the secret of its theme is unknown. Perhaps a note that he scribbled to himself on an airplane gives a hint: "The Lord was expressing something to us far greater than the simple words he spoke to some simple fishermen—understand that there is a God far greater than the mind of man can conceive." And he considered that every film since *Cleopatra* was becoming increasingly closer to a central conception he had had in mind, and his last project was to perhaps tie it all together and give the world his final message. That is where the mind of C. B. was probing the last few months of his life.

A close friend and associate, Donald Hayne, wrote of DeMille in a tribute: "He sought perfection in everything, from the details of his conservative meticulous dress to his creative work and his mind's outreach to the Divine. The perfection he sought often eluded him. But he was a man of unquenchable faith and hope and a courageous heart. Those near him have been saying to each other, these past few weeks, that they feel numbed more than sad, unable to believe that that heart failed at last. He was a man of vision. Now he sees."

Appendices

I

Vital Statistics

Full name:	Cecil Blount DeMille
Born:	August 12, 1881
Birthplace:	Ashfield, Massachusetts
Family home:	Washington, North Carolina
Parents:	Henry Churchill DeMille, playwright, partner David Belasco. Mathilda Beatrice Samuel, teacher, later founder DeMille Play Company and screenwriter.
Brother:	William Churchill DeMille, playwright, motion picture director; Professor of Drama, University of Southern California.
Family:	First American ancestor, Anthony De Mil, arrived in New Amsterdam from Holland aboard the *Gilded Beaver* on April 15, 1658; his son, Pieter, became Mayor of New Amsterdam. Another ancestor, William Blount, was a signer of the Constitution.
Boyhood:	Washington, No. Carolina; Pompton and Echo Lake, N.J.; New York City.
Schools:	Pennsylvania Military Academy, Chester, Pa.; American Academy of Dramatic Arts, New York.
Married:	August 16, 1902—Constance Adams, daughter of Judge Frederick Adams of Orange, N.J., Judge of the State Court of Errors and Appeals.
Children:	Cecilia Hoyt (Mrs. Joseph Harper), Katherine Lester (the former Mrs. Anthony Quinn) and sons, John Blount and Richard DeMille. Thir-

teen grandchildren; two great-grandchildren, sons of Peter Calvin DeMille and Mrs. Cecelia El Boughdadly, who are the children of Mrs. Harper.

Early career: Playwright, stage producer, one of the organizers of the Standard Opera Company; associate with his mother in the DeMille Play Company.

Films: Founder with Samuel Goldwyn and Jesse L. Lasky in 1913 of the Jesse L. Lasky Feature Play Company for which he was Director-General. Company merged in 1918 to become the present Paramount Pictures Corp. In 1924, established DeMille Pictures Corp. In 1928, joined Metro-Goldwyn-Mayer as producer-director; 1932, returned to Paramount as independent producer.

Radio: Producer, Lux Radio Theatre of the Air, June 1, 1936 to January 22, 1945. (Refusing to pay a one dollar political assessment levied by American Federation of Radio Artists because he did not believe it was right, he quit his $100,000 position with the radio network.)

Among other activities: Founder, 1919, Mercury Aviation Company, one of the first American airlines to carry air freight and passengers commercially on regularly scheduled runs (see *L.A. Examiner,* August 14, 1920) ; vice-president and chairman of motion picture loans for Commercial National Trust and Savings Banks of Los Angeles, which was purchased by Bank of Italy and later became Bank of America. President, DeMille Foundation for Political Freedom.

Among services: President of the Motion Picture Relief Fund; Chairman of the Motion Picture Division of the Community Chest of Los Angeles; served on board of Academy of Motion Picture Arts and Sciences and Council of Motion Picture Organizations (COMPO) ; three-times president Association of Motion Picture Producers. In 1938, declined nomination for United States Senator. First chairman of the Red Cross Donor Drive for motion picture and radio industries. Chief

Consultant on Motion Pictures to the U.S. Information Agency. American Cancer Society (Chairman, Los Angeles).

Among memberships: Lambs Club, American Legion, Sons of the American Revolution, The Wings Club, Prince of Orange Lodge #16, F. & A. M., New York City; Al Malaikah Temple, A.A.O.N.M.S., Los Angeles; honorary, German League of Human Rights; Screen Directors' Guild.

Awards and Honors:

ASSOCIATION OF MOTION PICTURE PRODUCERS. DeMille, three times distinguished by election to the office of president, was presented with a plaque "in appreciation of his successful and efficient administration of the Association's affairs."

AWARD OF ACHIEVEMENT FROM MOTION PICTURE DAILY to Lux Radio Theatre, selected by radio editors of the U.S. and Canada as the best dramatic program in Fame's annual Radio Poll.

ASSOCIATED MOTION PICTURES ADVERTISERS, INC., Thirtieth Anniversary Award.

BOXOFFICE (MAGAZINE) BLUE RIBBON—Best Picture of the Month, *The Story of Dr. Wassell.*

WAR AGENCIES OF THE GOVERNMENT OF THE U.S. for outstanding service in World War II.

AMERICAN CANCER SOCIETY—Distinguished Service Award.

PARENTS MAGAZINE AWARD for 35 years devotion to research in the production of historical pictures culminating with his greatest achievement, *Samson and Delilah.*

ACADEMY OF MOTION PICTURE ARTS AND SCIENCES—special award for 37 years from *Squaw Man* to *Samson and Delilah;* best picture, *The Greatest Show on Earth*: Irving G. Thalberg Award.

AMERICAN LEGION CITATION for 37 years of outstanding leadership in the motion picture industry.

GRAND PRIX, FILM FRANCAIS, for *Samson and Delilah.*

PHOTOPLAY MAGAZINE ACHIEVEMENT AWARD for *The Greatest Show on Earth.*

DAVID WARK GRIFFITH MEMORIAL FOUNDATION. First Annual Citation.

LOOK MAGAZINE AWARD—Best Picture of the Year—*The Greatest Show on Earth.*

BRAZILIAN ASS'N OF MOTION PICTURE CRITICS—Scroll in "Homage . . . for his good services to the Cinema the World over."

"GEORGE"—GEORGE EASTMAN HOUSE AWARD for Distinguished contribution to the Art of Motion Pictures 1915–1925—Festival of Film Artists Medal of Honor.

LOOK MAGAZINE MOVIE AWARD—for "outstanding achievement in producing *The Ten Commandments.*"

PHOTOPLAY MAGAZINE AWARD—for "creation of one of the screen's greatest emotional and religious experiences, *The Ten Commandments.*"

BOY SCOUTS OF AMERICA, LOS ANGELES COUNCIL—On his 76th birthday, "In recognition of his unflagging interest in the nation's youth . . . his indomitable spirit—that same which made possible the growth of this nation which he has so effectively served."

ADULT EDUCATION COUNCIL OF DENVER—citation—"For his unique and imaginative contribution to the university of Education and Understanding by giving a new dimension to great classics of world literature through the medium of the Motion Picture . . ."

THE AMERICAN ACADEMY OF DRAMATIC ARTS, from which he was graduated in 1900, Award of Distinction.

ORDER OF HOLY SEPULCHRE, from Patriarch of Jerusalem.

ORDER OF ORANJE-NASSAU, from Queen Wilhelmina of Holland.

COMPANION TO THE ORDER OF THE WHITE ELEPHANT, Thailand.

GRAND ORDER OF THE REPUBLIC OF ITALY, President Giovanni Gronchi.

CHEVALIER OF THE LEGION OF HONOR, France.

MEDAL AND DIPLOMA, City of Paris.

HONORARY DEGREES—University of Southern California, Doctor of Fine Arts; Pennsylvania Military College, Doctor of Letters; Brigham Young University, Doctor of Letters; Baylor University, Doctor of Letters; Temple University, Doctor of Laws.

PHI BETA AWARD, Excellence in Speech Arts.

NATIONAL SCHOOL BOARDS ASS'N., "outstanding service to education."

SCHOOLS NAMED IN HIS HONOR—Cecil B. DeMille Junior High School, Long Beach, California; Cecil B. DeMille Grammar School, Westminster, California.

U.S. TREASURY DEPT., U.S. Savings Bond Program.

U.S. AIR FORCE, highest award to a civilian.

CIVIL AIR PATROL, "distinguished service to aviation."

U.S. CHAMBER OF COMMERCE, "Greatest Living American."

SCREEN PRODUCERS' GUILD, Wreath of Honor.

SCREEN DIRECTORS' GUILD, David Wark Griffith Award.

EXHIBITORS LAUREL AWARD, Foremost producer-director, yearly since poll founded 1948.

GEORGE FOSTER PEABODY AWARD, Lux Radio Theatre.
BROADCAST PIONEERS, "contributions to . . . radio and television drama . . . for high standards established."
FOREIGN PRESS ASSOCIATION AWARD, "Master Showman."
GRAND LODGE, FREE AND ACCEPTED MASONS, STATE OF NEW YORK, distinguished achievement medal.
AL MALAIKAH TEMPLE, SHRINE, LOS ANGELES, "for bringing honor and pride to the nobility."
SALVATION ARMY, "Man of the Year—1958."
RELIGIOUS HERITAGE OF AMERICA, "Lay Churchman of the Year—1958."
CHRISTOPHER AWARD, *The Ten Commandments.*
B'NAI B'RITH AWARD, "significant achievement."
FEDERATION OF MOTION PICTURE COUNCILS, *The Ten Commandments.*
GENERAL FEDERATION OF WOMEN'S CLUBS, *The Ten Commandments.*
DAUGHTERS OF THE AMERICAN REVOLUTION, *The Ten Commandments.*

There is considerable controversy about many pictures which were made at Lasky Features and later at Paramount that Cecil B. DeMille was supposed to have codirected, or at least assisted in the direction. The films, for which he does not get billing and which he does not mention in his rather extensive autobiography, are the following:

Brewster's Millions (Codirected with Oscar Apfel) 1914
The Master Mind (Codirected with Oscar Apfel) 1914
The Man on the Box (Codirected with Oscar Apfel and Wilfred Buckland) 1914
The Goose Girl (Codirected with Fred Thompson) 1915
Nan of Music Mountain (Codirected with George Melford) 1917
Don't Tell Everything (Codirected with Sam Wood) 1921
Chicago (Codirected with Frank Urson) 1928
Forgotten Commandments (Contained extracts from *The Ten Commandments*) 1932
Land of Liberty (Contained clips from 124 films selected by DeMille, included many of his own films) 1939
California's Golden Beginning (Directed the sequences featuring Earl Warren) 1948

II

Cecil B. DeMille and Actors by Charlton Heston

From the point of view of the Screen Actors Guild, one unique aspect of Cecil B. DeMille's production methods was especially valuable: his preoccupation with Hollywood as a production center. Of course, he did a few locations. The two pictures I acted in for him both had rather extensive locations away from Hollywood, one out of this country. *The Ten Commandments* shot nearly three months in Egypt, and *The Greatest Show on Earth* shot for weeks in Florida in the circus winter quarters, and on the road with the circus.

But with those exceptions, and of course the obvious locations required for some of his westerns, he shot nearly every foot of his films in Hollywood. Now this was not so surprising in the period when he was most active, the twenties and thirties, but it is quite unique today, and was through his later years. Rising production costs are, of course, a prime factor in the diminishing production picture in Hollywood today, but he always dealt with large budgets, and always brought it off.

The point is that DeMille hired a lot of actors and he hired them here. And he would keep them employed for long periods of time, which is useful from the Guild point of view.

With his long schedules, he liked to know that actors were available. He liked performers, not extras. To that end, he did something that is rare these days, and was indeed rare in his day. He would employ what amounted to a stock company of about a dozen utility players. This was true for both pictures that I did for him.

These were actors with no specific roles, but he carried them through the picture at, I suspect, scale. If a situation arose where

DeMille gifts an antique wax statuette of Andrew Jackson to Charlton Heston on the set of The Buccaneer, *1959.*

he wanted to give somebody a line, he didn't want to have to give it to an extra. During *Ten Commandments,* which shot for seven months, I know he employed some actors in that capacity who, figuring on a day player basis, made far more than I did. Which was fine with me; I was happy to have the part. But it was indicative of his generosity with actors.

At the same time, he had a reputation of being an ogre. I dare say it was well earned. I knew him only in his last years when he'd mellowed somewhat, but I'm told he used to be quite a Tartar. Even when I knew him, he'd have an assistant for breakfast every now and then. But he was seldom hard on actors. He was usually, remarkably, even elaborately, courteous to actors. He almost always addressed a company as "Ladies and Gentlemen." Even with extras, his personal manner was punctiliously courteous. He was formal in an

Charlton Heston as Andrew Jackson in the second version of The Buccaneer, *1959.*

old-fashioned way which I found very attractive, even though it was old-fashioned.

To visitors on the set, as well as actors, he had a highly developed sense of public relations. He was probably the best public relations man in motion pictures. Certainly there were few that knew as much about it as he did, or had a more unerring instinct in that area. He never forgot that his enormous success depended ultimately on the public buying tickets.

In the silent days, the early twenties, I'm told, he had bleachers built when they filmed outside so that the general public could watch the production. I believe he charged them twenty-five cents a head. He would've been glad to admit them free; that wasn't the point. It was a rapport, a relationship, an understanding that he sought to establish with the public. This practice disappeared until Universal resurrected it a few years ago to their own great profit. DeMille understood this years ago.

But there are problems for visitors on a set. Usually you can never see anything because the entire production crew is in front of you. The camera crew, the lights, the grips, the sound boom, all block the view. So in order to accommodate visitors to his sets, DeMille usually took special measures. During *Ten Commandments,* he had a series of benches built on a catwalk against one wall of the sound stage, perhaps thirty feet in the air, which held as many as fifty people. There were at least a dozen visitors at all times. He was tremendously aware of the need to communicate directly with his vast audience.

He had a large office staff, and I believe that every letter he received was answered with some care. He had four secretaries, each with different responsibilities. If you wrote a letter to DeMille, you got an answer. And if there was a reason for you to be on the Paramount lot, he didn't mind being introduced to you. He was always most kind.

Sometimes his assistants didn't think so. They were the ones that felt his wrath when things didn't go as they were supposed to. I remember he always used more assistant directors on a picture than anybody else. For one thing he could afford it; for another, his pictures were big and complicated and required it. And for another thing, DeMille wanted it. And what DeMille wanted, Paramount was only too happy to provide.

Charlton Heston as Andrew Jackson in The Buccaneer, *1959.*

On *Greatest Show* he must've had at least eight assistant directors. The usual complement on a big exterior picture is four: one first assistant, and three seconds. On his pictures there were three first assistants and five seconds. And these were the guys that felt the Old Man's real sting. I recall an occasion on *Greatest Show* when a train sequence didn't come off and he lined up all eight assistant directors in a quasi-military formation and spent five minutes chewing them out . . . resourcefully. Never repeating himself and never pausing for breath.

Once or twice I saw him rip up an actor, but this happened only when he thought the actor was loafing, or oddly enough, (and perhaps unfairly) if he thought the actor was a physical coward. Not that he expected actors to do everything they were pretending to do in the film, of course. But he himself was a very brave man, and if he decided that an actor was afraid to do things that DeMille knew to be within his capabilities, the Old Man would cloud up and fall down on him. I only saw this happen once or twice.

Normally, though, he reserved the rough edge of his tongue for the assistants and the technicians on the set, many of whom were hired with the full awareness that this was one of the conditions of

Vincent Price, Charlton Heston and John Derek in The Ten Commandments.

Heston watches DeMille direct a scene in Egypt for The Ten Commandments *(1957).*

the game. I think that he used his theatrical rages to make an impression on the actors without disturbing them directly. For example, if an actress was consistently late to the set each morning, he would not chew her out. He would instead chew out her hairdresser, ruthlessly, to the verge of tears. Obviously, this would have some effect on the actress, without a direct impact.

I also saw him more patient with an actor than I have ever seen a director, much more patient than I would have been. There was a bit player, a member of the stock company I mentioned above, on the circus picture, whom I saw blow more takes than I've ever seen an actor blow. He muffed 27 straight takes. I'll never forget the line. It was in a scene with me. He was supposed to come up to the window of the pay wagon where I was paying a farmer for a load of hay. The farmer said, "Hey, you gonna pay me all in silver?" (It was in fact a practice of circuses in those days to use silver dollars for a great deal of their cash transactions.) "That's the way we get paid," I replied, and pushed a stack of a couple of hundred silver dollars off

DeMille and Heston on their way up to the top of Mt. Sinai for a scene for The Ten Commandments.

the ledge of the pay window, whereupon the farmer caught most of them hurriedly in his hat, a few spilling to the ground.

Just then this roustabout came running up and said, quote, "Hey, Brad, Holly's spinnin' like a weather vane in a Kansas twister!" But somehow, the actor just could not get that line out. Finally, after two hours of takes, DeMille had to replace him. But during that time, he never spoke sharply to the man; he was infinitely patient. That was the other side of the "monster."

It was also common knowledge among the older actors and smaller part players in Hollywood, that if DeMille was shooting a picture between November and January, there would be a big scene scheduled with a lot of small parts which would be carried for two or three weeks just before Christmas. Again, this goes back to a freer, easier time when production costs weren't as high, but it was nonetheless his practice. There were many performers, some with enormous ability, some with less, who could count on work in a DeMille picture near the holidays. This was not unique to DeMille; John Ford does the same thing. But it was typical of him.

I was first introduced to DeMille when I came out to Hollywood from New York to work for Hal Wallis in a forgettable picture called *Dark City*. After the picture was finished, I was on the Paramount lot to a meeting and was leaving via the DeMille gate. It was not his private gate; anybody could use it. It just happened to be right next to the DeMille building and was so named, as well it should have been. In fact, Paramount could well have been called DeMille Studios because the profits from his films kept the company solvent, as witnessed by the sorry days it's fallen on since.

In any event, I was driving off the lot through the DeMille gate in a convertible with the top down and he was standing on the steps of his building talking to a coterie of assistants and secretaries. I saw him and he glanced at me, and I thought, well, I *have* met him, so I waved and smiled. He bowed and smiled back, and I drove on.

As was later reported to me, he turned to his secretary, who did *not,* as was popularly supposed, take down every word he said; but she did take down the things that he might want to remember. She was always at his side during working hours and had an uncanny instinct for what he might want to remember.

He asked her, "Who was that young man?" His memory for names and faces was not good at all, even when he was younger. And at this time, he was not a young man.

She flipped back through her notebook and said, "He's Charlton Heston, a young stage actor from New York. He's made one picture for Hal Wallis, called *Dark City*. You ran it three weeks ago. You didn't like it."

"I liked the way he smiled just now," he said. "We better have him in to talk about the circus picture."

His casting interviews I'm sure were unique; certainly in my experience. As far as I know it was a routine he invariably followed. He would never show anyone a script. If he was considering you for a part, he would ask you to come in. He had a huge, cluttered and quite fascinating office, about 25 feet across, and jammed with memorabilia, models and awards, paintings, props and all sorts of odds and ends having to do with his films. He would sit at the desk or walk about the room, pointing out story boards, development sketches, scene or set models or costume designs, while telling you the story of the picture from the point of view of your character. But he never pretended that this particular character was the main character.

He would never say, "I'm considering you for this part," or, "I'm told that you might be good in this, and possibly it may work out." He certainly would never have you *read* for a part. He would merely *talk* about it, which left you at a loss for a response. You couldn't say, "Well, I think I could do that," because the question had never come up. I never did figure out the proper tone to strike there. Through half a dozen interviews for the circus picture, and maybe the same number for Moses, all I could say was, "Certainly is interesting. Sounds like it would make a fine film." He would describe a scene or the climax and show you sketches, and you'd say, "Certainly sounds like it should work." What else could you say?

The touchy subject of your capabilities for the role never came up, but he was obviously forming his conclusion. He looked at films or TV programs you'd done; he would talk to his colleagues. But never directly with the actor. Perhaps weeks would go by without a word. And then your agent would get a call and you'd go in again. Finally when he'd decided, he would never call you and say, "I've

Heston, Henry Wilcoxon and C.B. take a refreshing swim in the Red Sea while on location in Egypt for The Ten Commandments.

Heston and DeMille ride camels to the top of Mt. Sinai.

decided to give you the part." He would call your agent, who would then call you and tell you to break out the champagne.

I'm not certain that my early film beginnings with DeMille influenced my career into the epic genre. It's certainly a persuasive idea, but not necessarily true because my whole experience was rooted in this area. I was trained on the stage in Shakespeare. My first part on Broadway was in Shakespeare, which is of course epic theatre. I guess I simply am more castable in this genre, a point that DeMille helped establish.

The epic genre is difficult to bring off successfully. DeMille was a master at it. There was always a tendency to look upon him in terms of "genius" and "colossal." His name became synonymous with "spectacle," a word he abhorred, as do I. His type of film, the epic, has fallen into disrepute in recent years, and understandably, because it's the easiest kind of film to make badly, or conversely the hardest to make well.

I'm sure that everyone will concede that the best motion pictures ever made have been epics, from *Birth of a Nation* to *Citizen Kane . . . Alexander Nevsky* to *Henry V*.

Epics are difficult because you have to make another time period in history, and another whole set of ethics, a matrix of behavior, plausible to a 20th century audience. Without denigrating in the least the quality of films like *The Graduate* or *Marty* which are indeed brilliantly made, I would suggest that it is easier to communicate the problems of a 1968 college graduate or a Bronx butcher than it is to effectively communicate the behavior or problems of an 11th century crusader, or an Elizabethan knight.

In the first place, a lot of actors feel uncomfortable, and even look uncomfortable, wearing anything but 20th century clothes. Not many actors handle period dialogue well. And God knows very few writers are capable of writing it. So you're faced with the problem in the epic film of suggesting another time when people didn't speak with the colloquialisms they use now. They spoke with colloquialisms, but they were different colloquialisms. You must also by inference suggest another language, sometimes a dead language. Egyptian. Latin. Visigoth. You can't simply use archaic English because too much of it is incomprehensible. This type of writing is the hardest in the world, and there are only a half dozen writers who can do it at all. And the number of actors who can handle it is not much larger than that. That is why, I think, that there have been so many lousy films in the genre.

Certainly the fact that I did *Greatest Show* and then *Ten Commandments* for DeMille did a lot to make me castable in films. It made me a marketable, bankable commodity, which is what a star career requires. But it also created a pigeonhole from which I make unrelenting and vigorous efforts to escape.

Mr. DeMille was also responsible for my being cast as Andrew Jackson in *The Buccaneer* which was directed by Tony Quinn. I had already played Jackson in *The President's Lady* for Sol Siegal at Fox in preparation for which DeMille had let me see *his* 1938 version of *The Buccaneer* to study the character. He also let me look at some research materials. He was very kind about it. In fact, he lent me a combination research item and good luck piece, a lovely little wax statuette of Jackson, about ten inches high, which I kept in my dressing room while we were shooting *President's Lady*. Afterwards, I duly returned it to him.

Five years later, he was planning to remake *The Buccaneer;* at the time I don't think it was settled to what extent he was planning to involve himself in the production. I still had one picture left on the contract that Paramount had purchased from Hal Wallis. I asked to

Heston chats with an Egyptian.

play Jackson in a cameo role to use up the remaining commitment. He thought it was a fine idea. (I must admit that this was one time I didn't have to go through the long casting procedure.) The intended cameo role, however, blossomed into a considerable part as the script developed. As additional recompense, he gave me the little wax statue of Jackson.

I found Tony Quinn a stimulating director, a talented man and a very sincere artist, even though the film didn't turn out. I believe it was difficult for him to work for DeMille, as it was probably difficult to DeMille not to direct a picture that he had planned from the start. A close associate of DeMille's, Henry Wilcoxon, produced it, and even though DeMille functioned as executive producer, he meticulously stayed out of it. He was hardly ever on the set. I don't think Tony could complain about his interfering in the picture's direction. The cutting, however, was under the Old Man's supervision.

Beyond filmwork, I had very little contact with Mr. DeMille. He was not an easy man to know well. On locations I frequently had dinner or lunch with him. I attended his Golden Wedding Anniversary but so did about a thousand other people. Although he must have given a lot of dinners, I was never a part of that. But, of course,

Heston as Moses.

by this time, he didn't have the energy he had when he was younger. There really wasn't much of a social life to share with him.

He always treated me marvelously, and, as far as I know, spoke of me generously. He gave me an enthusiastic recommendation to William Wyler for *Ben Hur*. I had just been working for Willy, so it is debatable whether his recommendation was crucial to my getting the role. But DeMille gave it.

I've never considered myself a Cecil B. DeMille actor. I've been fortunate in working for many remarkable men who have had a share in shaping my career. Still, if I had to pick one man as being central, it would be DeMille. If you can't make a film career out of two DeMille pictures, with a combined gross of about a hundred million, you'd better quit.

Actually, I've been very fortunate in commercial terms. I've been in two films which have grossed more than $60 million, *Ten Commandments* and *Ben Hur* and another film which grossed over $30 million, *El Cid*. *Greatest Show* grossed more than $25 million, and

Planet of the Apes will gross about $20 million. But out of these five pictures that have done better than $20 million, DeMille made two of them. That's rather significant.

Ultimately, *Ten Commandments,* which was undeniably DeMille's greatest success, will have been seen by more people than any other film I've ever made, or probably will make. It was an enormous role, like Christ—unplayable, really. It was beyond my capacities then, and it would be beyond my capacities now. I dare say it would be beyond Olivier's capacities. I could do a better job now than I could then. But any actor with the brains God gave geese would be able to say that about any role.

It was a very gutsy piece of casting on his part. I was very young, only 28. I didn't have a remarkable film reputation. The only reputation I had was that created by the other DeMille picture. In essence, he put the most expensive picture he'd ever made on my shoulders, and I was not very firmly established. He did have one great advantage: he didn't *need* a really big name. His own name on a marquee meant as much as any actor's he could put there; and he employed the industry's biggest from John Wayne, Eddie G. Robinson, to Gary Cooper and Jimmy Stewart, Barbara Stanwyck to Betty Hutton.

Heston poses with Michelangelo's famous statue of Moses in Rome's Chapel of St. Peter in Chains.

In the entire history of films, no director's name has ever meant as much as his did internationally. Perhaps Hitchcock. But I would say that even Hitchcock carries only a third of the drawing power of DeMille.

The point I'm making is that he wasn't taking as much of a risk as any other director would have had to. He knew that when the picture got down to the smaller theatres, all that was going to be on the marquee was DeMILLE'S *TEN COMMANDMENTS.*

During his deliberation in casting the role, somebody brought to his attention the startling resemblance between my face and that of Michelangelo's Moses in the Chapel of St. Peter in Chains in Rome.

It's true. The resemblance is unmistakable. The nose is broken in the same place. The cheek bones are the same. It's really curious how my face seems to belong in any century but my own.

DeMille studied many photos of Michelangelo's Moses. During the course of a visit to Rome, he made a special visit to the Chapel to view it in person. DeMille was that kind of man. It could well have been the clincher. Because Michelangelo's work is probably the finest realization of what Moses could have looked like, it couldn't help but influence him.

Somebody quoted him as saying, "If it's good enough for Michelangelo, it's good enough for me."

III

The Biggest Man I've Ever Known by Henry Wilcoxon

Cecil B. DeMille was a pioneer in every sense. He was responsible for a great many innovations, trends and milestones in the motion picture industry.

One example of his contribution came with the advent of talking pictures. When sound came in they had to put the camera into a soundproof booth because of the awful grinding noise it made. This was like caging a lion. DeMille felt terribly restricted. Unable to work like that, he told his cameraman to take the camera out of the booth and to wrap a blanket around it. You could still hear the noise. They wrapped it again. But the sound man insisted that it wouldn't work. C. B. called for more blankets. There was a man on the set, Norma Shearer's brother, who told him, "C. B., I think I know what you want. I can give it to you if you can hold up shooting till tomorrow." The next morning, Shearer had built this contraption out of blankets and chicken wire. It was unsightly but it worked. That was the first blimp.

There were many things of this nature that he brought along. He developed lighting techniques. In the old days, they just used flat lighting. But in shooting a scene with some people around a campfire, he just lit it from one side. His distribution office in New York screamed, "Why have you given us just half a picture? Nobody will pay for this." And so DeMille wired back, "Look here, I gave you a Rembrandt. For Rembrandts you pay double." So he really invented lighting effects.

If I remember correctly, he had the first independent studio in Hollywood, a barn on the corner of Selma and Vine. They used to

DeMille and Henry Wilcoxon.

shoot everything out in the open with crude white-material diffusers to cut the harsh shadows. That was their light. Everything was lit from above by God Almighty. But he wasn't satisfied because he wanted to be able to get under people's hats to see their faces. He and Mrs. DeMille went down to an old playhouse in town and borrowed some stage floodlights and shot them under the cowboy hats. Another of his firsts.

Also in the silent days when they were using the hand-held camera, he wanted to pan from downstairs to an upstairs window, but in a single take. He sort of balanced a long ladder on a fulcrum and had people hanging on one end of it and the other end went on up to the window. So I guess he invented the camera boom.

In the early days, many men invented the same things. The "Old Man," as he was called by many of his contemporaries, always gave credit to D. W. Griffith for being the "Father" of the Industry. Among other things, he said Griffith invented the closeup. And that Griffith was the first man to photograph thought, by being able to see, through a closeup of the eyes, the thinking of the actor.

Even so, DeMille was one of the first to use introspection. His picture "The Cheat" delved into psychological problems, as did his "The Whispering Chorus." These were both before 1920, and were well ahead of their time.

The major thing about DeMille was that he was the most accurate audience barometer I've ever seen. He knew better what the average man wanted to see than anyone else I've ever met in my nearly 50 years in the business. This was a quality shared with another great pioneer in show business, the late Walt Disney.

There was great admiration, respect and friendship between Disney and DeMille. Everytime Disney made a new picture he would send a print over to DeMille, and Mr. DeMille would do the same. The Cecil B. DeMille Award was appropriately given to Walt Disney in the Annual Golden Globe ceremony a few years back and I had the pleasure of presenting it to him.

Both Disney and DeMille appealed to the same broad family audience, although their work was different. There was a curious story around Hollywood that Disney once did a poster for a DeMille film, "Male and Female," I think. The story goes that Walt Disney brought the sketch of the poster to Mr. DeMille who thought it was all right, but it didn't have enough sex to it. So Walt, it is said, took the poster, which had been designed for a vertical with a man and woman on it, and laid it on its side, saying, *"How about that?"* DeMille bought it.

About five or six years ago I produced a TV special over at MGM called "The World's Greatest Showman." It was about DeMille and had such people paying tribute to him as Yul Brynner, Edward G. Robinson, Bob Hope, Cornel Wilde, Betty Hutton, Barbara Stanwyck, Rev. Billy Graham and others. It was really something. This was sponsored by Kodak as a Christmas Special.

I approached Walt Disney to see if he would help with it. At the time, *The Wonderful World of Disney* was also sponsored by Kodak, and NBC-TV wisely scheduled the show right after the Disney hour on Sunday night. Disney not only allowed us to shoot a sequence at his studio, but he insisted on paying for it. He also taped a two-minute on-the-air promotion film about how great DeMille had been, at his own cost. And then Disney took those two minutes and made room for it during his own show, asking people to stay tuned for the tribute to a great showman. It was one great showman honoring another.

Master showmen like a Disney or a DeMille don't die, physically

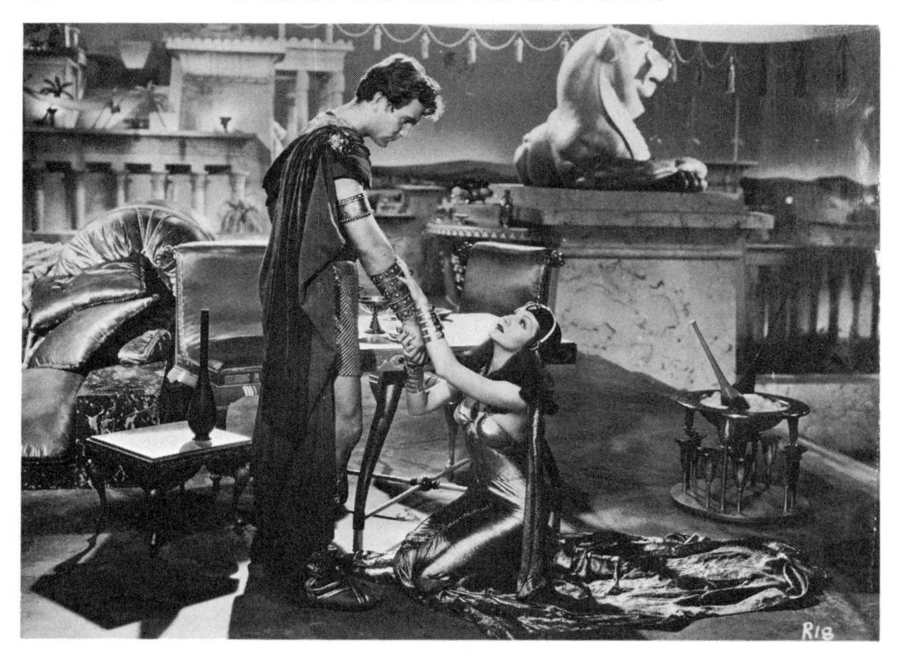

Claudette Colbert was DeMille's choice for Cleopatra.

yes, but not philosophically or spiritually. They are so powerful that their personalities continue long after they are buried. I find myself always using the present tense when speaking about Mr. DeMille. I don't say "He wouldn't have liked that," but instead say, "He wouldn't like that." And I don't do it consciously. He and I had a special relationship and he will be alive in everything I do as long as I am.

We first met when he was preparing *Cleopatra* for production. I had just finished starring in a successful play in London called *Eight Bells,* which had been seen by a Paramount Studio representative who arranged for a screen test to be made from the play. He sent the test to the Studio in Hollywood and I went under contract to them.

Their first step was to screen my test for all the contract producers and directors at the studio, informing them that I was a young English actor recently signed to a contract and was available for their use. On this particular day, DeMille was in the projection booth about to run some footage of horses he was going to use in *Cleopatra.* When he heard my voice on the test, he asked who I was. The projectionist told him. He said, "Very interesting voice," and looked

Wilcoxon and Loretta Young in these scenes from The Crusades. *Wilcoxon played Richard the Lion Hearted, Loretta the princess he loved.*

through the projection booth window into the projection room. "Never mind the horse footage," he told the projectionist, "run this test for me instead." After seeing the test, he announced, "There's my Marc Antony."

Cleopatra with Claudette Colbert was the first film I did in the States. The next was *The Crusades* with Loretta Young. Both productions seem to hold up today, *Crusades* a shade better even though he was freer with his historical facts in it. He readily admitted that he was interested in entertaining, not in giving a history lesson. He wanted only to capture the essential spirit of the Crusades, not dogmatically chronicle each one. Taking dramatic situations from different campaigns, he captured the essence of that colorful and boisterous age.

We immediately hit it off and I appeared in leading or main supporting roles in six of his twelve films since 1934. In 1943 I went into the service for five years as a gunnery officer on a destroyer. But the minute I got out I went back to DeMille. On *Samson and Delilah,* the second picture that we did after my return, he made me his associate producer as well as co-starring me in the film. We were very close friends and had genuine regard for each other professionally. I thought I could be of great service to him, which I was. I co-produced *Samson, The Greatest Show on Earth* and *The Ten Commandments.* My blood is on every frame of those three pictures.

He was a rough man to work for. If you delivered, you were okay, but if you didn't, you were fired quickly. And contrary to popular belief, he didn't like "yes-men." He would often say to his staff or to actors, who may have been yesing him, "Goddammit. Stand up for yourselves. I don't want fifty little DeMilles running around here. One is bad enough." He was a grand old man. You either hated him or loved him. There was no half measure. I happened to be one that loved him.

His physical discipline was quite rigid. He rarely smoked, except for an occasional pipe, and never on a set. He drank a bare minimum of alcohol, one drink in the evening. And during a business conference he wouldn't have a cup of coffee because he didn't want to miss a point. Although he was no athlete, he remained phenomenally healthy. He walked a great deal to keep in shape. Inadequacy of any sort, and that meant his own body as well, was unacceptable to him. His personal regimentation was kept up even through his later years.

Many people criticized him for wearing his boots and riding breeches on the set because they thought that he was putting on an

Wilcoxon poses next to a statue of the real King Richard.

act. True, he was extremely showmanship conscious, but there was utility in his choice of clothes. He wore boots because his feet and legs needed the support. He would get tired much more quickly if he didn't wear them, and if he were tired, he felt that he couldn't give his best to the production.

It was for the same reason that a boy followed him with a chair everywhere on the set. He rested for brief spells during the long day. It was important to him to conserve his energy for the great pressures of directing.

He was a supreme perfectionist, like Walt Disney. And like Disney he made it clear that he was the captain; he was in total command. But at the same time, he would listen to anybody, the grips, electricians, visitors. If you didn't agree with something, he expected you to come up and say so. He would then try to break your argument down, bantering back and forth. If there was an impasse, he would say, "Let's do it my way." And once he decided, his attitude became one of "Now shut up. Don't waste time. We're doing it my way." But until a decision was made, he actively solicited opinions of people on the set.

Also, if someone who was not on his immediate staff happened to be in the screening room, he wanted their opinion. "Don't tell me what you liked about it," he would say, "tell me what you didn't like." He would constantly question people to keep in touch with popular tastes. He always questioned taxi drivers, for example.

Trying to please as many people as he obviously did, he was bound to come up with touches of hokum at times. But in the films of yesterday, the good ones as well as the bad ones, there was a lot of corn. The old pictures sometimes tended to become formularized. But there were different kinds of corn. If it's big tough old field corn, it's hard to stomach, but if it's golden bantam corn, it's okay. DeMille consistently came up with golden bantam. Certainty was golden.

More people have seen DeMille pictures than any others in the history of the world. He was in the business of producing for the masses. Also in the business of making, but the latter never seemed to be the most important thing to him. He always took that for granted. His main concern, again like Disney's, was entertainment. He said so, often.

DeMille was a man who didn't change his mind on the basics of what he was making films for. As a person, he changed all the time. He was one of the most inquisitive men I've ever known, and it kept him vital and dynamic. If his ticker hadn't blown up on him, he would still be going and developing as a person, giving new dimension to his work.

The basic precept that he never wavered from was that the most important thing in production is the *story,* and for a successful story you have to have strong conflict. He always had more than one writer. He used to get all his writers together for storming sessions. For example, on *The Greatest Show on Earth,* he assembled his writers and told them that he wanted a one-liner on paper of what the picture was going to say. "And the first of you gentlemen," he added, "that mentions the words 'circus' or 'big top' is fired. I don't want that at all. Tell me a story about people, a very basic story, which could be dropped into a fish cannery, a studio . . . or a circus. First I want the plumbing in this house and a strong foundation. Don't write me a lot of beautiful trimmings. Don't start putting curtains up before the windows are built."

DeMille was a great one on dramatic construction. This is another characteristic he had in common with Mr. Disney. He would write as much as any of the writers. I know a number of people who say that he was unsubtle in the way he approached his work. But he was making a certain commodity for a certain market. Somewhere in the early stages, he would say to his writers, "All right, let's do a Jody version of the story." He would ask me to explain to those who hadn't heard of the Jody version before. He had a grandson, Joseph, whom they called Jody. And at the time this system was inaugurated, Jody was about seven. It seems that DeMille was having trouble with the current story. It was getting messy and complicated. He finally said, "Write me two pages and not more than three pages of what this show is about. I'm going to take it home and read it to Jody. If he starts squirming, it's no good." The object was to write a Jody version in simple terms. Jody didn't like that particular one. And the Old Man asked him what he didn't like and the boy pointed to something that proved to be a fault in the plot. A character hadn't been properly motivated and therefore didn't ring true to the child. DeMille continued to use this technique long after Jody had grown up. It was very important to him that everything in his work ring true. If it could be reduced to simple terms and still hang together, then it was sound.

This passion for ringing true motivated him as a director. Perhaps that's why his crowd scenes were the most realistic ever put on film. When he did the crowd scenes for *The Ten Commandments* for example, he told the mass of extras: "Ladies and Gentlemen, I just want to say one or two things to you about the scene that you are going to play." After describing the scene, he would say, "I don't want any extras on my set. I want actors and that is what I believe I hired when I engaged you for this picture. Now I'm warning you that if while we're doing a scene, whether in the marketplace or whatever, and you have a specific thing to do which the assistant directors will give you, I want you to be able to tell me, if I should ask, just exactly what it is that you are doing. I'm also warning my assistant directors. If I get to you and ask what you're doing and you can't tell me, then you and the assistant are immediately fired. However, you might tell me that you have your little son there and that you're taking him across the marketplace to have his sandal mended, but you better have a sandal that needs mending. And I want you to be able to tell me why you're going so fast with the child, and if you can tell me that the reason is that you have to have the sandal mended

DeMille directing third version of The Squaw Man. *Note the muffled camera and microphone.*

quickly in order to be home in time to fix your husband dinner, that's good. If you can't tell me some such thing, you're fired and your section assistant director is fired. Remember, I don't want any extras."

It made them feel like they were doing something. Like they were really part of the show. They weren't like the crowds you see in most pictures today where everyone has the same expression and is aimlessly moving around at the same speed. A real crowd of real people isn't like that. They're more like a DeMille crowd. They were actors not extras.

In handling stars like Gary Cooper and Barbara Stanwyck, the Old Man would for the most part leave a scene to them. If there was something he didn't like about their interpretation, he would discuss it with them. But he hired them as actors and expected them to do the job. He realized that an actor knows more about the character he's playing than anyone else, except perhaps the writer. He would guide the actor in an interpretation, but before any shooting began. An actor for a leading part was usually brought in for lunch, and before receiving a script, DeMille would tell him the story from that particular character's point of view. As if that character were the hub of the whole thing. After the actor had his script and production began, DeMille expected him to be on time and to know his lines. Sometimes he would ask the actors to stay after shooting for the day was done to run through some upcoming scenes to make them smooth. And then the next morning, everything went easily. One of the most important and valuable things to him, one that would always spell success, was preparation.

Contrary to what I would have expected of him, sometimes he found it difficult to make decisions. He would sometimes drag his feet until the last minute. Often, when he did, he was right. He threw a lot of the casting in my lap. Sometimes we would lose an actor because he wouldn't make up his mind, but often a better actor would come along.

I was valuable to him for many reasons, but mainly for two things. I could sketch and this helped him to visualize scenes, sets, costumes, camera angles and that sort of thing. And secondly, I could evaluate things quickly and give my opinion. He wouldn't always act on my opinions, but he did often enough.

Although he would sometimes be slow in decision-making, he could act quickly in an emergency situation. In the old days the stage lights would occasionally blow up like a bomb. The first time I heard one go off, simultaneously DeMille yelled "Look down!" and no one got any glass in their eyes.

His normal working day began in the early morning hours. He'd work at his home office till noon when not shooting a picture and then come to the studio for lunch with his staff of about twelve or fourteen people. We'd all been there since 9 A.M. and he'd be fresh. Those luncheons were actually conferences. He often said that no matter what subject came up, there was someone on his staff that knew something about it.

He would then work through the afternoon and be one of the last to leave. A few of us would usually wait for him to go first. I always did because he would often give me a final decision on a single matter in that last minute before leaving the studio. I would catch him in his car about to drive off the lot and he'd say, "Phew, what a day," dismissing everything from his mind. Then I'd hit him with one more idea, one more thought. A single thing that needed a decision. He'd be able to give me an answer because everything else was put out of his mind and he was relaxed. He knew he was being manipulated, but it rather amused him. I got more final decisions from him at that particular time of the day than practically all of the rest of the time together.

Rarely, very rarely, he would make a decision that I couldn't accept. Mostly it was putting his work before his health and well-being.

I was with him when he killed himself little by little in Egypt. We had set up two cameras high atop a wall to film a spectacular crowd scene for *The Ten Commandments* and he wanted to check something that wasn't working out properly. So he climbed the 94-foot ladder to the top of the gate where the cameras were. I was right behind him and couldn't get off the ladder because he began to sway above me. I got up there finally and his face was bright green. He sat down looking away from the others and caught his breath. "I'm all right," he said. "Leave me alone." I told him that he had better not climb down. "Who the hell are you to tell me that I can't climb back down? How else am I going to go down?" I told him that we could rig up a bosun's chair on a pulley. His answer was: "Shut up Harry." You couldn't argue with the Old Man and so he climbed back down. In the meantime we had walkie-talkied for a doctor. His personal physician and the set doctor both came over immediately.

After running some tests on him, they discovered that he had torn a massive hole in his heart. They told him that they would put him in an oxygen tent and if he stayed there for about eight weeks and rested, he might live. "Forget it gentlemen, I'm going to the set in the morning," he replied. He wouldn't listen. I insisted that he couldn't go out to the set. We had rehearsed the shots that were scheduled and that I could handle them. He grew vitriolic: "Right now, Harry, shut up or you're fired." I said, "I don't care if I am fired, you can't go out there tomorrow." Then his daughter Cecilia took me by the arm and said, "*I'm* telling you to shut up Harry. If my father wants to kill himself, let him do it." He was on the set the very next day, and by some miracle his heart mended itself and he was able to continue for a little longer. He could have even lived longer but no one could change his mind or course once he'd set it.

DeMille was a painfully honorable man. He never did anything that was underhanded or sneaky. He was the biggest man I've ever known. I miss him. So does the Industry. The gates of Paramount Studios wouldn't be open today if he hadn't been there. Take away

A scene from Unconquered. *Victor Varconi as Captain Simeon Ecuyer, Henry Wilcoxon as Captain Steele (Ecuyer's second-in-command), Gary Cooper as Captain Christopher Holden, Paulette Goddard as Abigail Hale, Ward Bond as John Fraser and Virginia Campbell as Mrs. John Fraser (Half-Pint).*

the grosses of half-a-dozen pictures like *Samson and Delilah, The Greatest Show on Earth* and *The Ten Commandments* and that company would have gone under long ago.

The ironic thing is that for all of his contributions to the Industry, the film people in their idiosyncratic inadequacy failed to give him more than one Oscar. A quote from the Bible perhaps is appropriate: "A prophet is not without honor except in his own country." I think that there was a lot of personal and professional jealousy that prevented his being properly recognized like Disney was. He had a certain flamboyance that irritated many. Even though this flamboyance mellowed as he grew older, they still talked of him as the "bathtub king." They resented his building publicity and advertising hooks right into a picture. He knew what he was doing. You couldn't be associated with David Belasco, as DeMille was in his younger years, without some of his showmanship rubbing off. When DeMille was working he commanded more space in print than anyone else. Perhaps they resented this too.

True recognition for DeMille's greatness will come many years after his death, when his work proves its lasting quality.

IV

The DeMille Legend by Elmer Bernstein

During my association with Cecil B. DeMille, I saw him genuinely unhappy on only one occasion.

In these times when one is accustomed to seeing people wear their troubles and neuroses like distinguishing badges of honor; when the works of many modern artists are undecipherable unless you know their case histories: when self-expression has come to mean "I'm afraid you will have to tolerate my unbalanced behavior," it is really extraordinary to realize that in two years Mr. DeMille only once allowed himself the luxury of sharing hurt with his youngest colleague.

It was the morning that the nominations for the Academy Awards were announced in the Spring of 1957. *The Ten Commandments* had not been nominated in any of the major artistic categories with the exception of special effects, but the picture as a whole had been nominated as the picture of the year.

Apparently, the members of the Academy saw the picture as an act of God and were not willing to acknowledge any of the human achievements responsible for creating something they thought worthy of a nomination as the best motion picture.

I entered the Paramount lot by the so-called DeMille gate on that morning, and immediately ran into Mr. DeMille who was on his way to his office. I expected him to be in a towering rage, and was not too anxious to see him. But he saw me first and called out to ask me to join him in his office.

Elmer Bernstein with Mr. DeMille.

The memory of that office will always be indelible. Despite a widespread impression to the contrary that Mr. DeMille worked off-stage in Byzantine splendor as he did on-stage, it was a simple, smallish office. But with Mr. DeMille behind the desk and a whole history of the American motion picture almost carelessly strewn about in the form of old photographs, mementos and even a silent film projector in the anteroom, a vist to the office was an unforgettable experience.

On this morning, however, he did not sit at his desk but joined me in sitting on the couch. His first concern was that I might be disappointed for failing to be nominated for my work on the score. He told me that in his opinion I would be compensated in a grander way by living to see my grandchildren enjoy the music because he believed the movie would become a classic and be shown for many years to come.

I expressed dismay for his sake that the picture did not achieve the honor that he might have hoped for and in that moment I saw sadness in him for the first time. Instead of his characteristically incisive reaction to expressions of sympathy, he hesitated for a long moment and finally said, "I guess we will just have to be satisfied with the grand award of the peoples of the world at the box office."

I tell this story first because I think this is as close as one could come to the marvelously complicated man that was Cecil B. DeMille. His fantastic generosity, his unrelenting drive for perfection, his famous rages, and his life-long loyalties as well as his stubborn defense of certain individual rights growing outmoded in a highly organized and unionized society—all these are part of the legend. The artistic ambitions, the deep disappointments and even the joys were private and very few people were privileged to see them.

I was first invited by the head of the Paramount music department, Roy Fjastad, to try to write a dance that was needed to shoot a scene for *The Ten Commandments.* I used the word "try" advisedly because I was informed that the casualty rate among such composers could be quite high and that Mr. DeMille was a difficult man to please.

There was no question that he was surrounded by an aura of fear, and it was catching. By the time half a dozen people had tried to "interpret" Mr. DeMille for me, I was indeed nervous when I finally was ushered into his presence on the lavish set of an Egyptian Throne Room one afternoon. I had been given so much advice on what or what not to say or do, that I was not really prepared for the courtly, impeccably and conservatively dressed man who very quietly said, "I'm very happy you were able to join me here on the set as my time is somewhat limited these days," a wry joke.

He then proceeded to tell me that as nothing is known of how ancient Egyptian music actually sounded, he would like me to invent it on the basis of materials which would be made available to me by his research chief, Henry Noerdlinger. He would also like me to do for the Egyptian music what Puccini did with Japanese leitmotifs in *Madame Butterfly.* Did I think I could do that, he wanted to know. I replied that I doubted that either my ego or my talent was that great, but that I would certainly try to do my best.

With that, he dismissed me graciously and said he would see me on the scoring stage in one week's time. My informants told me he was impressed by my honesty (which, incidentally, was a quality that was always the quickest way to his respect), and then they proceeded to terrify me with injunctions to write melodically, to avoid the use of woodwind instruments and many other suggestions.

But I had decided to do just what he had asked, and when recording day came, the orchestra consisted of plinky things, bells, wooden

DeMille, always an active energetic director, shows Yul Brynner how to brandish a sword on the set of The Ten Commandments, *1956, on location in Egypt.*

flutes and other devices that would at least make sounds like ancient instruments. The first rehearsal horrified most of the advisers and when Mr. DeMille appeared on the stage the tension was palpable. He listened with no comment, asked to hear it once more, and then said, "Fine, thank you very much." It was as simple as that—when he liked something. I stayed on a week-to-week contract after that for a year.

After four weeks of unqualified success, I finally came to a cropper on a chant and was lacerated for my inability to understand what Mr. DeMille wanted. After he stormed out of the room, I remained at the piano, shaken. I asked Henry Wilcoxon, the associate producer, whether I was now expected to leave or what. He said that Mr. DeMille was being very kind to me compared to what he could say when he was really angry, and that what was expected of me was more intensive effort. Later that afternoon, I met Mr. DeMille as he was leaving the studio, and he chatted pleasantly about having heard that I had become a father again. He made no reference to my failure.

Only later did I learn that the work day indeed did come to an end for Mr. DeMille and regardless of what transpired during the course of the day I was always his "young friend, Mr. Bernstein" after hours. His innate manners and sense of dignity kept me on a "Mr. Bernstein" basis until I felt he knew me well enough (three or four months) to take the privilege of a first-name relationship.

Mr. DeMille seemed curiously reluctant to make a commitment assigning me, or any other composer, to do the full score of *The Ten Commandments.* My work consisted of writing music for dance sequences, and for a time I never knew whether next Friday, or the Friday afterward, would be my last on the job.

Finally, Roy Fjastad thought the issue should be settled and he told Mr. DeMille as much.

"Now, Mr. DeMille, what about Mr. Bernstein?"

"Do you think he is another Wagner?" countered DeMille.

Obviously he was not ready to make a decision, but he was leading up to it. He came to me and asked me if I would be willing to com-

John Carradine, Julia Faye, Charlton Heston, DeMille, Olive Deering and Nina Foch chat between scenes on the set of The Ten Commandments.

pose "elements" for a score—the elements consisting of themes for key characters, such as Moses and Rameses. I said I would.

Shortly afterward he ordered an audition, and brought with him a small retinue headed by Henry Wilcoxon, writers, and two secretaries. He valued the opinions of his secretaries because to him, they were the voice of the public—the box office public.

The audition became, in effect, an oral examination. As Mr. DeMille would call out the name of a character, I would respond by playing the corresponding theme I had composed. When he called for the Moses theme, I played a dignified sonorous passage I thought appropriate for that great patriarch of the Old Testament.

"That's all right, Mr. Bernstein, but what about Moses when he was a foundling baby in the bullrushes?"

I hadn't come prepared for Moses the infant, but I realized this might be a critical moment in my career with Mr. DeMille. I quickly improvised a Moses *lullaby theme*.

When I finished, Mr. DeMille turned to the secretaries.

"What do you think?" he asked.

The secretaries applauded, and that seemed to settle it.

"Mr. Bernstein, do you think you could stand me another six months?" and that was how my temporary employment on *The Ten Commandments* became permanent.

In the end, on the last Christmas of his life, he invited me into his office and I thought he looked tired. He was surrounded by many paintings of an artist he had been supporting. The paintings were lying in profusion, unframed. We didn't speak of work, or new projects, but of the paintings and the life of the artist.

He asked my opinion of the work, and was interested in which of the paintings I liked best. He asked about my children, and how things were going for me. I wished him a Merry Christmas and a Happy New Year, and left.

On Christmas morning, the painting I had admired arrived at my home, framed.

V

DeMille: Man and Myth
by Art Arthur

To me, Cecil B. DeMille was Hollywood's best known unknown. No one in show business ever operated over a longer period of time in a hotter spotlight. And no one on the Hollywood scene ever contradicted his own legends more consistently than he did as you got to know him better and better.

I joined his staff with one hand on the ripcord. As he related in his autobiography, I didn't want the job and had to be persuaded to take it. I had heard that he was a man-eater. At the first opportunity I said to him, "Mr. DeMille, I want you to know that my respect for you is exceeded only by my respect for myself." He looked at me baffled, as if wondering how it could be otherwise. I thought I'd test him again when he wasn't satisfied with something I had written and asked me to rewrite it. He read the rewrite, nodded, and said, "That's better." I said, "You mean *even* better." He loved it.

Naturally, I was aware of the "yes man" legend. I had challenged it on several notable occasions and found it wasn't so. I asked him about it. He snorted, "I can get 'yes men' for a great deal less than what I pay people around here." Then he added, "Including you!" What else could I say but *yes.*

He could be formidable. No question about it. But I saw secretaries tame him with a single twinkle of humor. My favorite anecdote about him, which has never before been in print, stemmed from his determination to have quiet on the set. He had explained

Mr. DeMille with Art Arthur.

to me the reason for his stern insistence: the hub-bub on a large set could make it necessary to shout even the most simple instruction to an actor only a few feet away. And he was impartial in banishing violators of the call for *quiet*. Once he ordered his own daughter off the set for talking after quiet had been requested during a rehearsal. Another time it was Hedda Hopper.

It was against this background that he found himself one day with a few minutes to spare between camera set-ups and unexpectedly decided to go to his office, where he seldom appeared during shooting hours. I was walking with him as he entered the long corridor of the DeMille bungalow, and started for his office at the other end. Doris Turner, one of his secretaries, looked up in utter astonishment —then couldn't resist it. She asked, "What happened, Mr. DeMille? Did you talk on the set?"

He could appreciate wit and display it himself with Shavian skill. I once asked him how many Oscars he had won. "Eleven," he answered, "but they only gave me three." And there was the night he was honored with the Milestone Award by the Screen Producers Guild. At the climax, the stars who had worked for him stood up, one by one until the entire ballroom seemed filled with glamorous standees. As the last introduction was made, every eye turned toward Mr. DeMille for his sentimental acknowledgement. He said, "I want to thank each and every one of you with all my heart for your great patience with me over the years." A vibrant second passed and then the place rocked as he added dryly, "Exceeded only by my patience with you."

One of his veteran crew members was asked if C. B. was as tough to work for as people said. He answered, "Not at all. All he wants is absolute perfection and a good day's work." He paused, thought about it and continued, "A very good day's work."

But the same crew member was on the list of people who were called together—completely out of the blue—as *The Ten Commandments* was reaching completion. The Old Man had something he wanted to tell them. He had personally observed that each and every one present had worked far and beyond the call of duty. He had, therefore, decided to give each of them a unique type of raise—a percentage of his percentage of the picture's profits!

Since that day each member of the group—cameramen, film editors, set decorators, script girls, publicists, whatever—has received sizeable sums that, in some instances, total five figures. But it wasn't the amount that counted. Chico Day, an assistant director, said it for the group: "Listen, even if it was only one buck, it's still one buck more than anybody else in show business ever gave."

There was the persistent rap that his only interest in the Bible was a buck, that the only reason he made films about the Bible was because they were highly profitable. The most recent snide repetition of this was, as I recall, in *Esquire*.

The truth was that DeMille was a deeply religious man, whose father had been a lay minister (as well as a playwright), and who was raised with the Bible as part of his daily life. He put a far higher premium on faith than on dogma. But belief was there. His personal faith in the Bible is what constituted the basic difference between the success of the films he made about the Bible and the failure of so many Biblical films made by others.

I saw this best illustrated as I watched the response of audience after audience to the scene in *The Ten Commandments* when the Voice of God is heard by Moses for the first time. Some scoffed, but to many others it was a profoundly moving experience, reaching to their deepest religious roots. What made it so moving to so many was that the scene had been just as deeply meaningful and moving to the man who put it up there on the screen and they sensed it.

That single scene of humility and revelation, in my possibly knowledgeable opinion, had more to do with the tremendous popular success of *The Ten Commandments* than the vast scenes of spectacle so many others would cite so quickly—the parting of the Red Sea and the Exodus among them.

This was the scene which first confronted us with the Crisis of the Sound Track Clicks. It's an odd story, but it left no further doubt about the scene's emotional strength and meaning. Unlike so many producers, DeMille did not sit in the middle of the audience at the first vital screenings of any of his films. Instead, he would walk some two-thirds of the way down the far aisle, turn and stand unseen in the wall-shadows where he could watch the faces of the audiences. He knew every frame of what was up on the screen and saw no need to watch that. It was the audience faces and reactions that he wanted to watch. I had adopted the same technique in the far aisle on the other side of the house.

After the first New York screenings at the Criterion, we were both disturbed about the same thing, strange clicking noises in the sound

C.B. presents Art Arthur with a gag cake during a farewell luncheon at the time he left the DeMille staff in 1958.

The White House, September 1950. Front row (l. to r.): Brenda Marshall, Ned Depinet, President Truman, Myrna Loy; 2nd row: Bill Holden, C.B., Harry Brandt, the New York exhibitor; 3rd row: Art Arthur, Abram F. Myers, Arthur Mayer, Abel Green. The photo was taken during a visit to the White House of a delegation from the Council of Motion Picture Organizations (COMPO).

during the *Voice of God* scene. We had heard them before in Salt Lake City, but thought the sound had been corrected. Charlie Moss had just installed brand new sound equipment in his theatre. He was positive there was no defect there. The film itself was checked. No clicking sounds. Yet, at the very next screening, we heard them again. And at the screening after that. Then the mystery was solved as one of us noticed a woman make a small private gesture in the shadows of her seat. Standing close by in the aisle, we were hearing a sound that was not coming from the screen at all. As the emotional impact of the scene took effect, many women were seeking their handkerchiefs. The faint clicking sounds which had puzzled us so much came as they snapped open their purses.

The Board of Education in a Los Angeles suburb decided that they wanted to name a new school after Mr. DeMille but one thing made them pause. They knew about his conflict with the labor chiefs stemming from his refusal to pay a political union assessment. They were afraid that the local labor leaders would veto any proposal to honor DeMille.

Because I had the confidence of friends on the labor side, I agreed to explore the matter in a very quiet way. Finally I was talking to the top labor voice in the area. "Name a school after Cecil B. DeMille?" He told me. "Sure. He's a helluva fighter for his principles and a great American. They couldn't pick anybody better. Tell them to go ahead. There'll be no squawk from us. But, Art, just one thing . . ." And then came the part that explains why legends so often obscure truth. "Don't ever," he added, "say we said so!" I guess it's safe to mention it now without the name.

But the greatest contrast of them all was that between the popular Hollywood impression of him as a sort of two-gun General Patton of picture-makers and the man himself in any personal meeting. He had an old-fashioned gallantry and courtliness which was the absolute opposite of what people expected.

My entire family was completely enchanted by him from the first time they met. And he seldom overlooked any of the niceties. My wife's birthday and his were just one day apart. Both were Leos on the astrologers' charts. Invariably, he remembered to send her flowers, and with a charming personal note. One year, the note said, "I wonder if Art knows how lucky he is to have a Leo at the office as well as at home." By then, I knew. . . .

VI

Excerpt from Book Three of *Bulls, Balls, Bicycles and Actors* by Charles Bickford

. . . my phone rang. The call was from Cecil DeMille and his first words were, "Hello Charles Bickford. Welcome to Hollywood."

Those few kind words made all the difference. My self-esteem was restored and I again had the world by the tail. After an exchange of amenities, he invited me to an open house Christmas party [1928] . . . in progress at his office on the MGM lot. I accepted, of course, and he said that a studio car would pick me up within a half hour.

The party at the DeMille bungalow was merry, but decorous.

. . . a sturdily built, sun-bronzed man came toward me with his hand extended in greeting and although I had never met DeMille, nor seen a picture of him, I knew that this must be he. The pongee sports shirt, well-tailored riding breeches, leather puttees and Napoleonic stride seemed to proclaim the fact that here was the director to end all directors. "My God," I thought. "It's an American Benito Mussolini."

Restraining a compulsion to give him the fascist salute, I grasped his hand. The man had a grip like a bear trap. I thought nothing of it, having shaken hands with powerful men before.

1929 lobby card for Dynamite.

Although he was smiling, I detected the glint of antagonism in his eyes. It was difficult for me to believe that a man of his position would resort to such an infantile method of intimidation but as the pressure continued, I realized that he was serving notice to me that he was king of the mountain.

I rose to the challenge and matching him smile for smile, I bore down. Unfortunately for DeMille, my own meat hook was an instrument of considerable power and my own smile broadened as the challenging glint in his eyes changed to one of respectful dread.

He quickly recognized that his force was not as irresistible as he had supposed and slackening his grip, pressed the charm button, becoming forthwith as gracious a host as could be desired.

After extending me a warm welcome, he introduced me to the gathering which was composed of writers, directors, technicians and a few actors, among whom were Joel McCrea, then a tyro, Carole Lombard, also a beginner, and Lon Chaney.

The latent antagonism between DeMille and me was particularly interesting to me because of the mutual respect and admiration we held for each other's talents.

I considered his work extraordinary. It could be argued that most of his pictures were without reality, logic or artistic expression. They were, nevertheless, put together with consummate craftsmanship. And considering the possibility that they were consciously made to appeal to the great mass of infantile intelligence, they were, in my opinion, indubitable masterpieces.

I hold no brief for conscious artistry, in the theater or on the screen. I believe in sound stories, clearly and logically written and honestly projected as well-constructed plays, or screen plays. I object to so-called aesthetic approval, or criticism of any artist's work.

In my estimation DeMille was in a class by himself. As there was only one P. T. Barnum, so there was only one C. B. DeMille. Beyond any argument, he was a great showman. And I believe it was his opinion that I was a great actor. . . .

On the day following a drearily nostalgic Christmas, DeMille called again. Via the studio publicity department, he had learned that January first was my birthday. In his most courtly manner he assured me that he would consider it a privilege and a pleasure if I would celebrate by being his guest of honor at a New Year's party to take place at his mountain ranch, Paradise.

I appreciated the gesture and accepted, with thanks. . . .

He asked if there were any specific wines or liquors I was partial to and topped the quiz by asking my preference in women.

Slightly startled but nonetheless intrigued, I answered facetiously, "Why, Mr. DeMille, your hospitality overwhelms me."

"Oh, come now, Mr. Bickford," and though his tone was jocular I sensed a challenge. "Don't tell me I've overestimated you." . . .

I rose to the bait. "It's not that, Mr. DeMille. It's just that you're the last man in the world I would have expected to concern himself about my sex preferences, and it throws me."

He chuckled, appreciatively. "Don't get *me* wrong, Charles. I strive to please. I want you to have a good time. Which is it to be—blonde, brunette, or redhead?"

"Make it one of each," I said, modestly. "All I ask is that they be dainty, feminine, shapely, beautiful, intelligent and passionate."

I scored a belly laugh. "That's a large order in more ways than one. I know of only one such pearl of great price and unfortunately she's already wearing a band."

"Heaven forbid that I should step on anyone's toes," I laughed. "But it might simplify matters if you just tag the three with my initials—C. B. That should prevent any clash of interests. Or should it?"

The conversation ended on a note of amiable hostility. My suspicion that the New Year's party had been a long-planned affair did not lessen my appreciation of DeMille's gracious gesture in terming it my birthday party. . . .

I looked forward to the party with great eagerness, and for two reasons. The first was the hope that our close contact over the week-end at the ranch might lead to better understanding of each other and consequent cooperation and accord during the making of the picture.

The second was because of my very human curiosity concerning the nature of the party. DeMille was reputed to be something of a sybarite. His reputation, our bald dialogue concerning feminine companionship, the secluded ranch in the mountains—all these factors added up to the possibility that the party might turn out to be one of the legendary orgies. . . .

Certainly it was an exciting prospect for a guy with a strong streak of Yankee Puritanism.

The day of departure arrived and I was ready and waiting when my phone rang at exactly three P.M. The awe-stricken voice of the operator informed me that Mr. Cecil DeMille's car was waiting.

Cecil B. DeMille was also waiting. And seated beside him in the glittering black town car were three gorgeous girls—one blonde, one brunette, and one red-head! All three were dainty, feminine, shapely and beautiful. I could only presume they were passionate and hope they were of reasonable intelligence.

Each of them wore a small blue ribbon on which was emblazoned in gold the letters: C. B.

With a flourish DeMille performed the introductions, referring to me as that distinguished, dynamic, he-man star of the Broadway stage. And with a gleeful twinkle in his eye, he sat back and watched for my reaction. . . .

"Mr. DeMille, I've got to hand it to you. You sure know how to judge a man. Your taste is impeccable. . . . But there's only one thing that bothers me, I'm wondering what you have to offer for the second night."

That wonderful clown, Red Skelton, couldn't have gotten a bigger reaction. Seldom have I seen a man laugh so heartily. . . .

I think that if we had really been kindred spirits, this moment would have given birth to a life-long friendship. His relief at finding me normal opened him up like a flower and for the rest of the trip he treated me like a long lost son. . . .

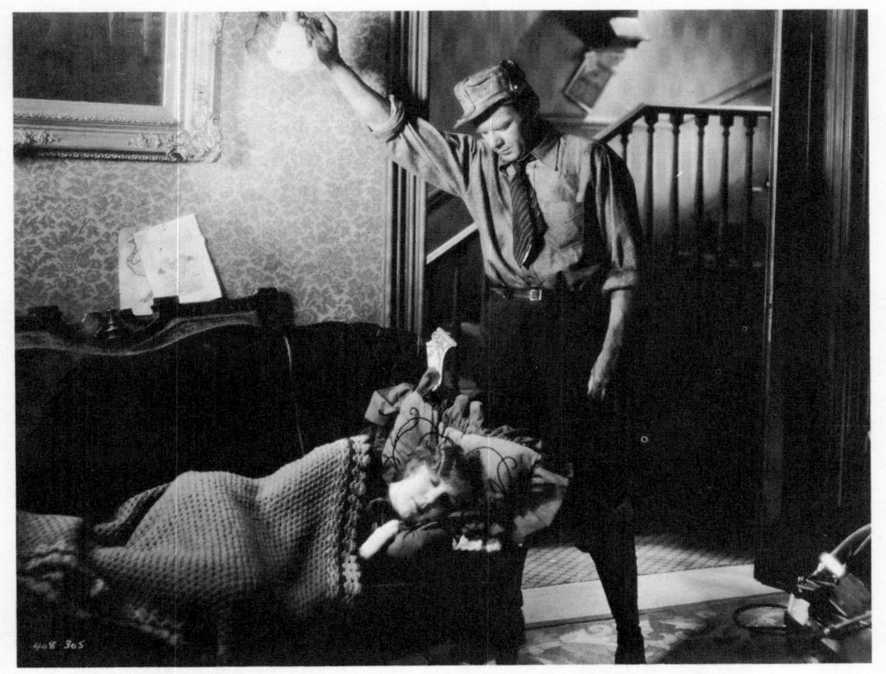

Charles Bickford and Kay Johnson in **Dynamite.**

DeMille was justly proud of Paradise Ranch. Nestling in a secluded mountain valley and but a few miles out of Los Angeles, it afforded everything it takes to make a perfect hideaway. I fell in love with it even before I saw it. As the car turned into DeMille's private road, we were suddenly engulfed in a subtle perfume, emanating from acres of lime, lemon and orange trees. This fragrance, blended with the sharp mountain air, made the simple function of breathing a sheer delight.

The road ended at the center of this enchanted forest, disclosing an attractive sprawling ranch house, a pool, handball and tennis courts.

Radiating from the major house were several shady lanes, or lovers walks, each leading to a picturesque little guest bungalow.

DeMille led us into a spacious living room, the salient features of which I remember as great comfortable-appearing divans and arm chairs upholstered in red leather, an enormous fireplace, and—most impressive in those prohibition days—a practical bar which boasted a breath-taking stock of pre-war liquors.

Exclusive of the staff of white-clad, Filipino house boys, there were some sixteen people present. I recognized a former Broadway matinee idol, a notorious swordsman who was equally famous for his portrayal of romantic roles and his facility at evading irate husbands. Also two screen *femmes fatale;* two hopeful juveniles, one quite manly; and several screen starlets, one of whom was destined to become a top-ranking star.

Here, certainly, was a high potential for orgiastic activity but after casing the joint carefully I reluctantly came to the conclusion that in decorum these people were indistinguishable from convivial groups I had dallied with at the Westchester Country Club. All were personable, gay, and believe it or not, engaged in animated conversations about many things, from cabbages to presidents.

I did not rule out the possibility of high jinks to come, however, particularly when, after the introductions, DeMille led me into the library where with great enthusiasm, he showed me his collection of erotica. I presumed it to be priceless and recognized that most of the volumes were beautifully bound and illuminated. Because of my

Kay Johnson, Conrad Nagel and Charles Bickford in action scene from Dynamite.

streak of inherent Yankee Puritanism, I suppose, erotica was to me synonymous with pornography and I was square enough to be embarrassed by it. I'm sure he was disappointed at my reaction.

I managed to display a modicum of phony interest by expressing admiration for a privately printed three-volume edition of shockingly illustrated works of Francois Rabelais. DeMille, in what I was to learn was a typical gesture, insisted that I accept it with his compliments. . . .

After rejoining the group it soon became evident that DeMille, true to his word, had designated me as the lion of the occasion. It was indeed my party and as it progressed I enjoyed myself hugely.

When at seven o'clock we were shown to our respective quarters to dress for dinner, I was in a mellow mood. My room was in DeMille's personal bungalow which consisted of a huge playroom and four spacious bedrooms; one for his personal use, the others for special guests.

I found my things unpacked and a Filipino house boy in attendance. Laid out on the bed were my dress trousers and a red silk Russian blouse. I looked at the thing in amazement and asked the house boy, "How come?"

He explained that it was Mr. DeMille's custom to have the male guests wear red blouses at dinner. "Very pretty," he volunteered.

"I should imagine so," I said. "What an eccentric idea. And what does Mr. DeMille wear?"

"Russian blouse," he answered. "Only always white, yellow or black."

It occurred to me that here was a perfect opportunity to pull another gag on the master. I instructed the Filipino to go to Mr. DeMille's room and tell him that I could not wear the blouse. "If he wants to know why," I said, "Tell him it's too small."

He reappeared shortly, accompanied by my concerned host. He explained that the blouses were tailored in three sizes—small, medium and large. The one in question was indubitably large. However, he politely accepted my statement and was about to send the house boy for another blouse when I interrupted.

"Don't bother sending for a red one. It would still be too small. The only Russian blouse that will fit me tonight must be white, yellow, or black."

For an instant temper flashed in his eyes. But remembering he was the gracious host and I the guest of honor, he favored me with a quarter smile and said seriously, "Please don't think I am arbitrary about this, Charlie, but it's traditional here at Paradise for my male guests to wear the red blouses at dinner. Put it on. You will find it very comfortable and you'll look stunning in it."

I continued in serious vein. "I'm sorry, C. B., I certainly have no wish to appear ungracious but that shade of red clashes terribly with my hair. Besides, as guest of honor, I think I should be allowed to co-star at the dinner table. Or, you go ahead and star solo in white, and I will settle for the feature spot in black."

The gag fizzled. He didn't dig my humor at all. But after a moment of serious consideration he decided my idea had merit. "Nice showmanship" he called it and sent for a black blouse.

It was not only becoming but comfortable; much more so than the conventional dress shirt and dinner jacket. The master went up a notch in my estimation. There appeared to be method in what I had deemed mere eccentricity.

Together we walked back to the main house, or perhaps I should say we marched. He always seemed to be leading a parade. During that short walk, in semi-darkness and with no one watching, I got the impression he was attempting to keep one pace ahead of me.

As we entered the house, or rather as we squeezed through the door side by side, the assembled guests broke into a round of applause. Evidently they had the impression we'd been racing and were ending up in a photo finish.

Dinner was served promptly. Several tables had been pushed together, forming a half circle before the great fireplace in which a log fire was now blazing. The flickering firelight, augmented by the mellow glow from dozens of candles, provided the only illumination resulting in a subtle change in the atmosphere of the great room. . . .

The dinner was a lively affair, with much gossipy conversation and goodnatured banter. DeMille, a superb host and skillful raconteur, saw to it that the ball was kept in the air; there were no dull moments.

In line with the general atmosphere, I had expected the menu to consist of a profusion of rare and exotic dishes. I couldn't have been more wrong. The *pièce de résistance* was corned beef and cabbage.

After dinner two teams were organized to play charades. I was chosen to captain one team. DeMille headed the other. The orgy image was receding into the dim distance. My Aunt Sarah used to throw wilder parties than this one, I thought.

Yet, champagne flowed like water and as the witching hour approached, some of the boys and girls developed a hot and bothered gleam in their eyes.

Charles Bickford and Kay Johnson in a scene from Dynamite.

"Of course," I reasoned. "It's New Year's Eve. Something other than corks will start to pop at midnight."

And so they did. But only in terms of noise and enthusiasm. There was an abundance of noise makers, tin horns and whistles and at twelve o'clock everybody cut loose. The din was terrific. . . .

Perhaps because by this time my vision was slightly out of focus, DeMille appeared to resemble old Bacchus himself as, surrounded by his votaries, he passed out long slim candles to the Bacchae.

He explained that they were called Brides Candles and according to old Spanish custom were to be used to foster the romantic spirit among the senoritas and caballeros. If a girl were in the mood for dalliance, she had but to light her candle and place it outside her door. The caballeros would take it from there.

Having expounded this quaintly naughty bit of folklore, he announced that he was about to retire to his quarters, making it clear, however, that the party was by no means over and that he would take it very unkindly if we allowed his absence to spoil the fun.

The revel continued but the spark was gone. With the great man no longer present, the necessity for impressing him was no longer existent. Within a few minutes, several of the guests drifted.

Someone turned on the radio and tuned in Ben Bernie's band,

broadcasting from Catalina Island. And so we danced, flirted, smooched and went through all the motions of having a gay old time. . . .

After about a half hour of this, the major-domo approached me and whispered that Mr. DeMille was expecting me at his bungalow. I welcomed the summons. My thinking was that DeMille wished to discuss *Dynamite* over a social nightcap. In my half-stewed condition, I saw nothing incongruous in holding a story conference at one o'clock of a bibulous New Year's morning.

But this man of constant surprises had again thrown me a curve.

I walked into his bungalow to discover that I had been called, not to a story conference but to a party. Or perhaps I should say to *the* party, for it was plain to be seen that this was the center ring; the star performers were assembled and the main show was on.

The big play-room was in semi-darkness except for a pool of light in the center, cast from the ceiling by an artfully concealed spotlight. A girl, beautiful, blonde and petite, was dancing. She was nude but for a diaphanous veil which she cleverly manipulated as she writhed, python-like, to the beat of Ravel's *Bolero.*

Three men: DeMille, the Broadway leading man, and one of the juvenile actors—the manly one—watched avidly as they sprawled on the carpet just outside the circle of light.

Three girls, the cream of the crop, catered to the gastronomical desires of the men from a table laden with a Lucullan display of food and drinks.

The performer was blessed with an exquisite body; she was a bumper and grinder *par excellence.* She finished to enthusiastic applause from all of us, but DeMille's fervor caused me to wonder if somewhere on her anatomy she wore a brand. In an effort to find out, I tried, unsuccessfully, to persuade her to encore without the veil. . . .

After the dance we played games. First, a marble rolling contest for prizes. Quite innocuous, but lucrative. I won an expensive Leica camera and a matched set of hammered silver flasks.

Then we engaged in a sort of strip-tease dice game. Very naughty but lots of fun, evidenced by howls of laughter from the men and squeals of outraged modesty from the girls as, piece by piece, the losers were forced to discard bits of clothing.

Luck was with me, or against me depending upon the point of view, and the game ended with me fully clothed surrounded by semi-nude nymphs and satyrs. It developed into quite a shindig and there were some cute capers cut. . . .

The group which came together in DeMille's office [several weeks later] consisted of DeMille, his entire staff of writers, technicians and assistants; the cast of *Dynamite* which included Conrad Nagle, Kay Johnson from the Broadway Theater, Carole Lombard who was then known I think, as Jane Peters, Joel McCrea, then a tyro, and myself.

We were all eagerly expectant and keyed up to the importance of the occasion. *Dynamite* was to be DeMille's first talking picture. It was the very first motion-picture venture for both Kay Johnson and me. It was a new medium also for most of the sound engineers and for the camera crew. . . .

After introductions, DeMille, very horsey that morning in riding breeches, tweed jacket and boots, conducted us into the big conference room where rows of folding chairs had been set up.

As we seated ourselves, DeMille, flanked by three scenario writers whose names I have mercifully forgotten, ascended a platform on which were his desk and throne chair.

The first assistant called for silence and DeMille began to speak. It was a masterly oration, comprising the complete history of his film career from its inception in a Vine Street barn where he'd given birth to *The Squaw Man* up to the momentous present in which a panting world waited to view his first masterpiece in the new medium of sound.

Then followed a commendably short lecture on togetherness, stressing the newness of sound and the consequent necessity for working as a team.

He spoke well. The talk was interesting, constructive and at times amusing.

So far, so good.

There was a pile of scripts on the desk. Picking up one of them, he read aloud the descriptive material concerning the three leading characters and the locale of the story.

At this point my expectation was that the scripts would be passed out so that we could go ahead with a reading rehearsal, such as I was accustomed to in the theater.

But he continued to read and had progressed well into the dialogue of the first sequence when Kay Johnson blurted to me, "My God! He's not going to read the whole script to us?"

Everybody in the room heard her. There was a ripple of laughter followed by a pregnant silence as DeMille, his face reddening with anger, glared down from the dais.

I was embarrassed for Kay, expecting her to be withered by a blast of devastating sarcasm.

I needn't have been. DeMille suddenly smiled and said graciously, "I'm sorry, Miss Johnson, I didn't quite catch what you said. You have a question?"

Kay was not one to be caught with her tail up. Returning smile for smile, she said sweetly, "No, Mr. DeMille. I was just saying to Mr. Bickford that it's wonderful of you to read for us. I didn't mean to interrupt you."

"Think nothing of it," he returned blandly, and resumed his reading.

My own reaction was neutral. I'd never known a producer to read a script to the cast, but I thought, if this is Hollywood procedure, so be it.

My complacency didn't last long.

The story began to emerge as a mish-mash of contrived situations, peopled with unreal characters and weighted down with dialogue so naive as to be ridiculous.

DeMille's reading was no help. He had been an actor in his younger days and if one was to judge by his stilted speech and ponderous emphasis upon points, his acting must have left plenty to be desired.

But his enthusiasm was magnificent and he blithely forged ahead, pausing at intervals to note the impact of this dramatic bomb upon his captive audience.

Most of the listeners were raptly attentive. But why was I so disappointed? Months previously, when DeMille had told me the story over long distance telephone, I had judged it a mess of corn and had, nevertheless and after careful consideration, committed myself to it. Nothing had changed. By this reasoning then, my criticism must be directed at the dialogue.

Having arrived at this conclusion, I thought back to the beginning of the story and in my mind played some of the scenes, improvising the dialogue. As I became absorbed in these thoughts, DeMille's voice receded from my consciousness . . .

I was most embarrassed when I woke up. A grinning assistant director, having shaken me awake was standing by my shoulder while DeMille, smiling benignly at the delighted assemblage, said humorously, "It appears that the gentleman from the Great White Way is feeling the impact of our Hollywood night life." Then, after the resulting laugh, "Rough night, Mr. Bickford?"

"Something like that," I said contritely. "I'm sorry."

"Do you feel quite rested now?"

"Quite. Thank you."

"Sufficiently so that we may expect your attention during the remainder of this rehearsal?"

"I hope so."

"You're sure it's not too much to ask?"

"Positive."

In spite of the fact that his jocular manner had held the barb of sarcasm, I felt that he had handled the situation in true princely fashion.

He resumed reading and as this was the pre-coffee-break era, continued without interruption until the end. The reading had taken three hours. The script may not have been a good one but no one could say it wasn't a thick one.

The boys and girls gathered around the master and there was oh-ing and ah-ing as they congratulated him for his rendition of a great script.

The only abstainer was—guess who.

Feeling singularly awkward and conspicuous, I turned to make what I hoped would be an unnoticed exit. But the lynx-eyed DeMille stopped me in my tracks. "We still have to hear from our distinguished leading man," he said. "How about it, Mr. Bickford? Are you pleased?"

Flushed with pleasure at the enthusiastic reaction to the script, it was obvious that he sincerely believed in it himself and was expecting to hear words of praise from me.

I was embarrassed for both of us.

Arranging my face into what I hoped was a pleasant smile, I took a stab at diplomacy.

"Fine, Mr. DeMille. Just fine. Very exciting. What a story."

He beamed like a little boy being handed a lollypop. "I'm delighted. Coming from you, that's praise indeed." Then, to the others, "Mr. Bickford is a perfectionist, He's dedicated to the theater and is quite skeptical about us here in Hollywood. As a matter of fact, it took a lot of persuasion to induce him to leave his beloved Broadway. Now that he's here I hope he will be with us for a long time to come."

Then, as the scripts were being passed out, he said, "If there are any suggestions, I'd appreciate hearing them now as there will be no time for changes after we begin shooting."

C.B. discusses scene with Muriel McCormack and Charles Bickford (Dynamite).

Not caring for the position of having burned my bridges, I said, "I have a few points but I'd like to discuss them in private, if you don't mind."

He was not a subtle man. The smile became fixed and his voice was edgy as he said, "We're all working together here, Mr. Bickford, and are interested in one objective—to make a great motion picture. So don't be afraid to speak up."

He stepped from the dais and as he approached me, I caught the now-familiar glint of antagonism in his eyes. His very proximity exerted a juggernaut effect and seemed to pose the challenge—"Back up or be flattened."

My hackles began to rise.

"There is no question of my being afraid, Mr. DeMille. I just thought it might be wiser for me to speak my piece in private. I'm quite concerned about the dialogue."

"An interesting comment, particularly in view of the fact that it was written by the three highest paid writers in Hollywood."

"What you pay them is none of my business, Mr. DeMille. My concern is with the material they have turned out. In my estimation some of it is unplayable."

At this point, the male member of the writing trio, highly incensed by this attack upon his work leaped to its defense. "What are you talking about? This script was tailored to your measure."

"Then you must have used a lousy yardstick."

"And just who are you to make such a judgment? This is to be your first picture, isn't it? What do you know about picture scripts?"

DeMille silenced him with a gesture. He had no intention of allowing anyone else to cut me down.

"Mr. Bickford, you're out of order. I have been producing motion pictures for many years, successful motion pictures. And I know what I am saying when I call this an excellent script."

I was suddenly weighted down by a nascent foreboding of disaster. I was probably about to end a short and unhappy film career without having made a picture. But the die was cast. The dogs of war had been loosed and my Irish was up. . . .

"Understand me, Mr. DeMille, I am not criticizing the construction of this story. I don't even know enough about screen writing for that matter. But I've been writing and acting in stage plays for many more years than you've been producing motion pictures. And this dialogue stinks." . . .

DeMille's eyes narrowed to slits.

"He's measuring me for the kill," I thought, and tried to think of a good exit line.

But the expected explosion didn't occur. It was averted by the intervention of one of the women writers. Her voice dripped venom as she shrilled, "Mr. Bickford has a reputation for this sort of thing. He tries to rewrite everything he plays in."

He resented the intrusion. "I'm well aware of Mr. Bickford's reputation," he snapped. "That's why he's here."

By comparison, his tone was almost gentle as he turned again to me. "Pretty harsh criticism, Mr. Bickford. But if something smells that bad to you there must be a reason. I'll have to ask you to be more explicit."

"The words are completely false," I said. "Particularly to the characters of Cynthia and Hagon." (These were the roles to be played by Kay Johnson and myself.) "For instance in the bedroom sequence, the words the writers have put into their mouths are ludicrous. Those two people would not talk like that."

"You're sure of that?"

"Positive."

"I see. And just how, in your expert opinion, would you have them talk?"

Luckily I was a facile ad-libber. I picked up a script and started to read the sequence, improvising dialogue to fit the situation. It sounded pretty crude even to me and when I finished I fully expected to be blasted by sarcastic invective.

But this chameleon had changed color again. He was beaming like a benevolent Santa Claus. "That sounded pretty good. I'll really have to admit it sounded pretty good. Anyway, it's an improvement."

Turning to the three glowering writers, he asked, "Don't you agree?"

Obviously they did not agree, but knowing which side of the bread the jam was on, they nodded their assent as DeMille knew they would.

He then dismissed the rehearsal, asking the writers, his secretary and me to remain for further discussion. During the ensuing couple of hours, I sympathized with the writers as, fairly oozing hatred of me, they sat and took notes while I improvised dialogue.

I dismissed the incident as of little account but distorted versions of the story soon began to reverberate from the Hollywood Hills. Charlie Bickford had said "no" to Cecil DeMille. A myth was spawned . . .

A few days following the reading, *Dynamite* went into production and for months thereafter I was engaged in intensive, fascinating, and sometimes ludicrous activity. . . .

A few minutes before nine o'clock [on the first day of shooting] the stage door was flung open and the uniformed guard announced, "He's coming."

"Who's coming?" I asked of the nearest person.

"God. Who else?" was the laconic reply.

Irreverent people, those studio workers.

In spite of myself I was caught up in a kind of breathless anticipation as I awaited the Advent.

And it needed but little imagination to hear the sound of trumpets

Bickford in closeup.

as, a moment later, the demi-god of the flickers swept through the door.

Three paces behind him and in near-military formation were his assistant director, unit manager, film cutter, script clerk, megaphone bearer, chair bearer and secretary.

As he marched across the stage in my direction, I found it difficult to decide whether I should genuflect, laugh or applaud.

These derisive thoughts were quickly overpowered by a grudging admiration for the aplomb with which he carried out his ostentation. Not even now after years of intermittent association can I say for sure whether his pomposity was dictated by a sincere belief that he was to the manner born or by a magnificent flair for showmanship.

That first working morning, for instance, I watched in fascination as he mapped out the mechanics of the first scene. Every move he made found the script clerk, chair bearer and megaphone bearer moving with him like shadows, always but an arm's length behind him. They were trained to anticipate his every wish. If he wanted his megaphone, he had merely to extend his hand and it would be immediately placed in his grasp. If he were about to sit, he didn't look to see if the chair was there. He just sat. . . .

The first scene was one in which I, about to be executed for a murder which I did not commit, say "Goodbye" to my nine-year-old sister. Needless to say, Sis and I love each other very, very much and the scene as written was pretty mawkish stuff. What happened next I wouldn't believe except that it happened to me.

I was in my dressing room awaiting the call to rehearse when suddenly all activity on the set abruptly ceased. I heard the first assistant call for, and get, utter silence. From somewhere came the sound of music—soft music, and played with consummate feeling. A spinet player and a fiddler were pulling out all the stops as they played the tried-and-true old tear-jerker, *Hearts and Flowers.*

A minute later an assistant director rapped discreetly on my door and in hushed tones said, "We're ready for you, Mr. Bickford."

Responding immediately, I blithely walked onto the set where everyone, including the crew, stood with doleful expressions and bowed heads. Putting two and two together, I jumped to the conclusion that a gag was being pulled on me because of the sentimentality of the scene I was about to play. And, I thought, a very funny gag.

Going along with the joke I struck a pose and began to declaim, "Friends, Romans, countrymen, lend me your ears. I come to bury Caesar . . ." but stopped abruptly as I caught the shocked look of disapproval on DeMille's face.

Instantly contrite, thinking I had inadvertently been flippant at the expense of some memorial rite, I attempted to make amends. "Oh, I'm sorry," I said. "I didn't realize. *Has* someone died?"

From the resulting roar of laughter from the listening group, I realized even before the flush of anger crept up and over his high forehead, that I had made a *faux pas* and had only succeeded in shoving my foot farther down my throat. He was really concerned at my flippancy and explained in solemn tones that the music—and I swear by the beard of my sainted grandfather that I'm telling it straight—was necessary in order to create in me the proper degree of emotional intensity demanded by the scene.

Coming from the top producer-director of his time and delivered to an actor of my experience and standing, his statement was hardly to be taken seriously. Once again I suspected a rib. "You have to be kidding," I said.

Once again I was wrong. He was painfully serious. "I never joke where my work is concerned, Mr. Bickford. And that's what we're here for, to work. I have found that music is of material help in creating a mood."

Since to some extent we all use individual methods to obtain results and as this musical gimmick appeared to have worked for him, I was bound to respect it. On the other hand it could not possibly work for me, inspiring in me as it did nothing but derisive mirth. As I did not wish to be rude, insulting, or even mildly disrespectful, it was up to me to come up with an intelligent refute. . . .

"It occurs to me, Mr. DeMille, that most of the actors you have directed during your long and illustrious career were silent screen stars. Right?"

"That's correct. Although I've worked with many stage actors."

"You were once an actor on the legitimate stage, weren't you?"

"I was."

"Then perhaps you will agree that we of the stage have a different approach to acting than the people of the silent screen."

"I don't follow you."

"To put it bluntly: if the time ever comes when I need this type of stimulus to make me act, I will go back to swinging a pick for a living."

This brought forth a general laugh in which he joined. He was sporting enough to concede my point. The musicians were dismissed and we settled down to the business of making the picture. . . .

Shooting on *Dynamite* continued for several weeks. In spite of the constant rumors of pitched battles between us, DeMille and I had achieved a genuine respect for each other's abilities and were working smoothly together. We had even progressed to the point of addressing each other as "Charlie" and "C.B." Occasionally we had differences of opinion, differences which were promptly solved and promptly forgotten as being all in the day's work. But each unimportant incident, however, was distorted and inflated by the sensation-hungry journalistic leeches that were feeding on Hollywood's life blood, and each became part and parcel of a kind of Bickford myth.

There were a couple of serio-comic incidents that are worthy of note; at least, they still amuse me.

One day, for instance, Kay Johnson and I were working out a scene in which she was supposed to smash a bottle over my head. I, as a rough and virile character, disregard the blow, pick her up and carry her into a bedroom. During rehearsals, Kay was worried about the bottle business until DeMille, to reassure her that there was no danger of harming me, showed her one of the prop bottles. They were break-a-ways and made of transparent candy. But Kay remained skeptical so DeMille, bottle in hand, smilingly turned on me.

"How about it, Charlie—do you mind?"

"Be my guest, C. B.," I answered, trustingly.

"Now, watch carefully, Kay. I'm going to hit him as hard as I can."

So saying, he hauled off and let me have it.

No glass bottle could have been more lethal than that candy one. The property department personnel were realists. It didn't break.

When I came to, my prone figure was surrounded by worried people frantically striving to bring me back to the land of the living.

Kay, hysterical with laughter, was being helped to her dressing room.

There were a few malicious wags around the studio who insisted that DeMille had deliberately planned to do away with me . . .

In those early days of sound, the recording equipment was installed in sound-proof booths built into walls overlooking the sound stages. It was the practice for a director, after rehearsing a scene to his satis-

Judith Allen and Charles Bickford live it up in This Day and Age.

Charles Bickford as he appeared in This Day and Age.

faction, to retire to the booth where he could listen to the recorded dialogue during a final rehearsal.

On one occasion Kay Johnson and I were rehearsing a scene which she was having difficulty in playing to DeMille's satisfaction. The situation called for her to deliver a blistering tongue-lashing and DeMille felt she was not sufficiently virulent. We went through the scene several times with DeMille growing more impatient by the minute. Finally, he felt that the scene was ready to shoot and retired to the sound booth to listen to a final rehearsal.

Everything was proceeding splendidly when Kay suddenly fluffed a line. We stopped. Kay apologized and then DeMille, his voice booming over the loud speaker, waxed gently sarcastic. "That's all right, Miss Johnson. Don't let it bother you. Our production cost is only fifteen thousand dollars a day. Now, would you like a few hours to study your lines or shall we try a take?"

Kay, of course, was badly flustered, but good trouper that she was laughed it off and answered to the effect that she would like to try a take.

Everything was readied, the camera rolled and we started the take. The scene played beautifully up to the same line Kay had fluffed before. Then, as I was speaking her cue, I saw the panic rise in her eyes and knew she was going to blow it again. And she did. She sounded as though she had a hot potato in her mouth.

There was a moment of deathly silence. Then the master spoke. Through the speaker came a blast of sarcasm, biting sarcasm—belittling, humiliating and uncalled for.

Kay was hurt and slightly bewildered. Her eyes filled with tears.

I was angry for her. "Why do you take it?" I demanded.

"What else can I do?"

"Tell him off, for Pete's sake! Get mad. Tell the son-of-a-bitch to go to hell."

She didn't answer and for a long moment the big stage was as silent as a tomb.

DeMille broke the silence, his voice rasping through the speaker. "Miss Johnson . . ."

"Yes, Mr. DeMille."

"You're holding us up."

If Kay had hackles, I'm sure they were rising at this point. Her voice had the flavor of Tarragon vinegar. "I don't know what you're talking about, Mr. DeMille. What do you mean by that? I'm right here, ready and waiting. I haven't left this set for one moment."

"I'm aware of that, Miss Johnson. I can see you very plainly. I can also hear you. Both of your voices register very clearly. I'm waiting in case you care to follow Mr. Bickford's kindly advice."

This revelation of microphonic eavesdropping wowed the crew. I didn't think it was quite that funny. Neither did Kay. She was getting madder by the second.

DeMille supplied the last straw. His tone was now benign. "I'm still waiting, Miss Johnson."

Kay, stout lass, picked up the gauntlet. Her voice trembled with emotion. "You don't have to wait any longer, Mr. DeMille. You can start any time. You go to hell."

Surprisingly enough, no one laughed. The men on the set had the sensitivity to realize that Kay might be in for a most unpleasant time and their sympathies were with her.

I placed my arm around her and waited for the bolt to fall.

It didn't. Instead, the first assistant called for a take and the camera began to roll.

Kay didn't fluff this take. She was magnificent. All the wrath she had built up against DeMille was loosed upon me during the scene, with gratifying results. The scene was perfection. The crew favored us with a round of applause.

Afterwards, DeMille descended from his aerie and in his most masterful fashion, came striding onto the set where Kay and I waited for the battle to join.

But this remarkable man was not in a war-like mood. Quite to the contrary. His eyes were twinkling with good humor and his grin was cherubic as he approached us, his arms out-stretched to clasp Kay in an embrace.

"Kay, darling. You hit it right on the button," he said. "That was a beautiful scene, just beautiful. You were both great."

Then, taking from his pocket two twenty-dollar gold pieces he handed one to each of us, saying impressively, "Those are DeMille medals. They are only awarded for what I consider magnificent performances." . . .

He turned to me and said, "My double thanks to you Charlie, for your psychological assistance. I assume, of course, that you *were* being constructive."

"Of course, C. B., of course," I answered hypocritically, "and my thanks to you for your understanding appreciation."

And so the incident came to a happy conclusion, effectively giving the lie, I think, to those who insist that Cecil DeMille lacked a sense of humor.

VII

Film List and Credits

1913: THE SQUAW MAN—Lasky—from a play by Edwin Milton Royle. Adapted by Cecil B. DeMille and Oscar Apfel. Co-directed by Oscar Apfel.
CAST: Dustin Farnum, Winifred Kingston, Redwing, Dick La Strange, Foster Knox, Monroe Salisbury, Joe E. Singleton, Billy Elmer, Fred Montague, Baby de Rue, Dick La Reno.

1914: THE VIRGINIAN—Lasky—from a novel by Owen Wister.
CAST: Dustin Farnum, Winifred Kingston, Billy Elmer, Monroe Salisbury, Anita King, Tex Driscoll, Jack Johnstone.

1914: THE CALL OF THE NORTH—Lasky—from a novel "The Conjurer's House" by Stewart Edward White.
CAST: Robert Edeson, Theodore Roberts, Winifred Kingston.

1914: WHAT'S HIS NAME—Lasky—from a novel by George Barr McCutcheon.
CAST: Max Figman, Lolita Robertson, Sydney Deane, Fred Montague.

1914: THE MAN FROM HOME—Lasky—from a play by Booth Tarkington and Harry Leon Wilson.
CAST: Charles Richman, Theodore Roberts, Mabel Van Buren, Anita King, Fred Montague, Monroe Salisbury.

1914: ROSE OF THE RANCHO—Lasky—from a play by David Belasco, Richard Walton Tully and Cecil B. DeMille.
CAST: Bessie Barriscale, Jane Darwell, Monroe Salisbury, Dick La Reno, J. W. Johnstone, Jeanie MacPherson.

1915: THE GIRL OF THE GOLDEN WEST—Lasky—from a play by David Belasco and Cecil B. DeMille.
CAST: Mabel Van Buren, Theodore Roberts, House Peters, Anita King, Sydney Deane, Billy Elmer, Jeanie MacPherson, Raymond Hatton, Dick La Strange.

1915: THE WARRENS OF VIRGINIA—Lasky—from a play by Wm. C. DeMille.
CAST: James Neill, Mabel Van Buren, Blanche Sweet, Page Peters, House Peters, Marjorie Daw, Gerald Ward, Dick La Reno, Raymond Hatton.

1915: THE UNAFRAID—Lasky—from a story by Eleanor M. Ingram and Cecil B. DeMille.
CAST: Rita Jolivet, House Peters, Page Peters, Billy Elmer, Larry Peyton, Theodore Roberts, Marjorie Daw.

1915: THE CAPTIVE—Lasky—from a story by Cecil B. DeMille and Jeanie MacPherson.
CAST: Blanche Sweet, House Peters, Page Peters, Jeanie MacPherson, Theodore Roberts, Billy Elmer.

1915: THE WILD GOOSE CHASE—Lasky—from a play by Wm. C. DeMille.
CAST: Ina Claire, Tom Forman, Lucien Littlefield, Helen Marlborough, Raymond Hatton, Theodore Roberts.

1915: THE ARAB—Lasky—from a play by Edgar Selwyn adapted by Cecil B. DeMille.
CAST: Edgar Selwyn, H. B. Carpenter, Milton Brown, Billy Elmer, Gertrude Robinson, Sydney Deane, Theodore Roberts, Raymond Hatton.

1915: CHIMMIE FADDEN—Lasky—from a play by E. W. Townsend—adapted by Cecil B. DeMille.
CAST: Victor Moore, Raymond Hatton, Mrs. Lewis McCord, Ernest Joy, Anita King, Camille Astor, Tom Forman.

1915: KINDLING—Lasky—from a play by Charles A. Kenyon—adapted by Cecil B. DeMille.
CAST: Charlotte Walker, Thomas Meighan, Raymond Hatton.

1915: MARIA ROSA—Lasky—from a story by Guido Marburg & Wallace Gillpatrick.
CAST: Geraldine Farrar, Wallace Reid, Pedro de Cordoba, Ernest Joy, Anita King, H. B. Carpenter, James Neill.

1915: CARMEN—Lasky—from the novel by Prosper Merimee—adapted by Wm. C. DeMille.
CAST: Geraldine Farrar, Wallace Reid, Pedro de Cordoba Billy Elmer, H. B. Carpenter, Jeanie MacPherson, Anita King.

1915: TEMPTATION—Lasky—from a story by Hector Turnbull.
CAST: Geraldine Farrar, Pedro de Cordoba, Theodore Roberts, Elsie Jane Wilson, Raymond Hatton.

1915: CHIMMIE FADDEN OUT WEST—Lasky—from stories by E. W. Townsend—adapted by Cecil B. DeMille.
CAST: Victor Moore, Camille Astor, Ernest Joy, Mrs. Lewis Mc-

Cord, Raymond Hatton, Tom Forman, Florence Dagmar.

1915: THE CHEAT—Lasky—from a story by Hector Turnbull.
CAST: Fannie Ward, Sessue Hayakawa, Jack Dean, James Neill.

1916: THE GOLDEN CHANCE—Lasky—from a story by Cecil B. DeMille and Jeanie MacPherson.
CAST: Cleo Ridgley, Wallace Reid, H. B. Carpenter, Ernest Joy, Edith Chapman.

1916: THE TRAIL OF THE LONESOME PINE—Lasky—from a play by Eugene Walter and John Fox Jr.—adapted by Cecil B. DeMille.
CAST: Theodore Roberts, Charlotte Walker, Earle Fox, Thomas Meighan.

1916: THE HEART OF NORA FLYNN—Lasky—story by Hector Turnbull—adapted by Jeanie MacPherson.
CAST: Mario Doro, Elliott Dexter, Ernest Joy, Lola May, Billy Jacobs, Margaret DeMille, Charles West.

1916: THE DREAM GIRL—Lasky—from a story by Jeanie MacPherson.
CAST: Mae Murray, Theodore Roberts, James Neill, Earle Fox, Charles West, Mary Mersch, Mrs. Lewis McCord.

1917: JOAN THE WOMAN—Cardinal Film Corp.—from a story by Jeanie MacPherson.
CAST: Geraldine Farrar, Wallace Reid, Theodore Roberts, Charles Clary, Hobart Bosworth, Raymond Hatton.

1917: A ROMANCE OF THE REDWOODS—Artcraft Pictures Corp.—from a story by Cecil B. DeMille and Jeanie MacPherson.
CAST: Mary Pickford, Elliott Dexter, Charles Ogle, Tully Marshall, Raymond Hatton, Walter Long, Winter Hall.

1917: THE LITTLE AMERICAN—Artcraft Pictures Corp.—from a story by Cecil B. DeMille and Jeanie MacPherson.
CAST: Mary Pickford, James Neill, Ben Alexander, Guy Oliver, Edith Chapman, Jack Holt, Raymond Hatton, Hobart Bosworth, Lillian Leighton.

1917: THE WOMAN GOD FORGOT—Artcraft Pictures Corp.—from a story by Jeanie MacPherson.
CAST: Geraldine Farrar, Raymond Hatton, Hobart Bosworth, Wallace Reid, Theodore Kosloff, Walter Long, Charles B. Rogers, Olga Grey.

1917: THE DEVIL STONE—Artcraft Pictures Corp.—from a story by Beatrice DeMille and Leighton Osmun—adapted by Jeanie MacPherson.
CAST: Geraldine Farrar, Wallace Reid, Tully Marshall, Hobart Bosworth, Lillian Leighton, H. B. Carpenter.

1918: THE WHISPERING CHORUS—Artcraft Pictures Corp.—from a novel by Perley Poore Sheehan—adapted by Jeanie MacPherson.
CAST: Raymond Hatton, Kathlyn Williams, Edythe Chapman, Elliott Dexter, Noah Beery, Guy Oliver.

1918: OLD WIVES FOR NEW—Famous Players Lasky—from a novel by David Graham Phillips—adapted by Jeanie MacPherson.
CAST: Elliott Dexter, Sylvia Ashton, Wanda Hawley, Florence Vidor, Theodore Roberts, Helen Jerome Eddy, Marcia Manon, Julia Faye, Parke Jones, Edna Mae Cooper, Gustav Seyffertitz, Tully Marshall, Lillian Leighton, Maym Kelso.

1918: WE CAN'T HAVE EVERYTHING—Famous Players Lasky—from a novel by Rupert Hughes—adapted by Wm. C. DeMille.
CAST: Kathlyn Williams, Thurston Hall, Elliott Dexter, Sylvia Breamer, Wanda Hawley, Sylvia Ashton, Charles Ogle, Tully Marshall, Theodore Roberts, Ernest Joy, Billy Elmer, James Neill.

1918: TILL I COME BACK TO YOU—Artcraft Pictures Corp.—from a story by Jeanie MacPherson.
CAST: Bryant Washburn, Florence Vidor, Gustav Seyffertitz, Winter Hall, Clarence Geldert, George Stone, Julia Faye, Lillian Leighton.

1918: THE SQUAW MAN—Paramount-Artcraft—from a play by Edwin Milton Royal.
CAST: Elliott Dexter, Thurston Hall, Katherine McDonald, Helen Dunbar, Winter Hall, Ernest Joy, Herbert Standing, Julia Faye, Theodore Roberts, Noah Beery, Ann Little, Raymond Hatton, Jack Holt, Monte Blue, Pat Moore.

1919: DON'T CHANGE YOUR HUSBAND—Artcraft Pictures Corp.—from a story by Jeanie MacPherson.
CAST: Elliott Dexter, Gloria Swanson, Lew Cody, Sylvia Ashton, Theodore Roberts, Julia Faye, James Neill.

1919: FOR BETTER FOR WORSE—Artcraft Pictures Corp.—from a story by Edgar Selwyn—adapted by Jeanie MacPherson.
CAST: Gloria Swanson, Sylvia Ashton, James Neill, Elliott Dexter, Tom Forman, Wanda Hawley, Theodore Roberts.

1919: MALE AND FEMALE—Paramount—from a play "The Admirable Crichton" by Sir James Barrie.
CAST: Gloria Swanson, Thomas Meighan, Lila Lee, Theodore Roberts, Bebe Daniels, Julia Faye, Raymond Hatton, Robert Cain, Edward Burns, Wesley Barry, Mildred Reardon, Maym Kelso, Edna Mae Cooper, Lillian Leighton, Sam Searle.

1920: WHY CHANGE YOUR WIFE?—Artcraft Pictures Corp.—from a Wm. C. DeMille story adapted by Olga Printzlau and Sada Cowan.

CAST: Gloria Swanson, Thomas Meighan, Bebe Daniels, Theodore Kosloff, Sylvia Ashton, Maym Kelso, Lucien Littlefield, Edna Mae Cooper, Jane Wolff.

1920: SOMETHING TO THINK ABOUT—Paramount—story by Jeanie MacPherson.
CAST: Elliott Dexter, Claire McDowell, Theodore Roberts, Gloria Swanson, Monte Blue, Theodore Kosloff, Julia Faye, Mickey Moore.

1921: FORBIDDEN FRUIT—Famous Players Lasky—story by Jeanie MacPherson.
CAST: Clarence Burton, Agnes Ayres, Kathlyn Williams, Theodore Roberts, Winter Hall, Theodore Kosloff, Forrest Stanley.

1921: AFFAIRS OF ANATOL—Famous Players Lasky—from a play by Arthur Schnitzler—adapted by Jeanie MacPherson, Beulah Marie Dix, Lorna Moon and Elmer Harris.
CAST: Wallace Reid, Gloria Swanson, Elliott Dexter, Bebe Daniels, Agnes Ayres, Monte Blue, Wanda Hawley, Theodore Roberts, Julia Faye, Theodore Kosloff, Polly Moran, Raymond Hatton.

1922: FOOL'S PARADISE—Famous Players Lasky—from a story by Leonard Merrick—adapted by Beulah Marie Dix and Sada Cowan.
CAST: Dorothy Dalton, Mildred Harris, Theodore Kosloff, Conrad Nagel, Clarence Burton, Jacqueline Logan, Kamuela Searle.

1922: SATURDAY NIGHT—Famous Players Lasky—from a story by Jeanie MacPherson.
CAST: Edith Roberts, Jack Mower, Sylvia Ashton, Leatrice Joy, Conrad Nagel, Edith Chapman, Julia Faye.

1922: MANSLAUGHTER—Paramount—from a story by Alice Duer Miller—adapted by Jeanie MacPherson.
CAST: Leatrice Joy, Thomas Meighan, Jack Mower, Julia Faye, Jack Miltern, Dorothy Cummings, Edythe Chapman, Lois Wilson.

1923: ADAM'S RIB—Paramount—from a story by Jeanie MacPherson.
CAST: Anna Q. Nilsson, Milton Sills, Pauline Garon, Theodore Kosloff, Elliott Dexter.

1923: THE TEN COMMANDMENTS—Paramount—from a story by Jeanie MacPherson.
CAST OF THE PROLOGUE: Theodore Roberts, Charles de Roche, Estelle Taylor, Julia Faye, Gino Corrado, James Neill, Lawson Butt, Clarence Burton, Pat Moore.
CAST OF THE STORY: Edythe Chapman, Richard Dix, Rod La Rocque, Leatrice Joy, Nita Naldi, Robert Edeson, Charles Ogle, Agnes Ayres.

1924: TRIUMPH—Paramount—story by May Edington—adapted by Jeanie MacPherson.

CAST: Leatrice Joy, Rod La Rocque, Victor Varconi, Theodore Kosloff, Charles Ogle, Robert Edeson, George Fawcett, Julia Faye, Spottiswood Aiken, Zazu Pitts, Raymond Hatton, Alma Bennett, Jimmie Adams.

1924: FEET OF CLAY—Paramount—from a novel by Margaretta Tuttle—adapted by Beulah Marie Dix and Bertram Millhauser.
CAST: Vera Reynolds, Rod La Rocque, Julia Faye, Ricardo Cortez, Robert Edeson, Theodore Kosloff, Victor Varconi.

1925: THE GOLDEN BED—Paramount—from a novel by Wallace Irwin—adapted by Jeanie MacPherson.
CAST: Lillian Rich, Henry B. Walthall, Vera Reynolds, Theodore Kosloff, Robert Cain, Rod La Rocque, Warner Baxter, Robert Edeson, Julia Faye.

1925: ROAD TO YESTERDAY—Producers Distributing Corp.—from a play by Beulah Marie Dix and Evelyn Greenleaf Sutherland—adapted by Jeanie MacPherson and Beulah Marie Dix.
CAST: Joseph Schildkraut, Jetta Goudal, William Boyd, Vera Reynolds, Trixie Friganza, Casson Ferguson, Julia Faye, Clarence Burton, Charles West, Charles Clary.

1926: THE VOLGA BOATMAN—Producers Distributing Corp.—from a story by Konrad Bercovici—adapted by Lenore J. Coffee.
CAST: William Boyd, Elinor Fair, Victor Varconi, Theodore Kosloff, Julia Faye.

1927: THE KING OF KINGS—Producers Distributing Corp. Scenario by Jeanie MacPherson and DeMille, no credit to DeMille. Assistance from Denison Clife, Clifford Howard and Jack Jungmeyer. Based on the Gospels of Matthew, Mark, Luke and John.
CAST: H. B. Warner, Dorothy Cummings, Joseph Schildkraut, Rudolph Schildkraut, Ernest Torrance, Jacqueline Logan, Julia Faye, Majel Coleman, William Boyd, Sojin, Joseph Striker, Clarence Burton, Josephine Norman, Mickey Moore, Muriel McCormick.

1928: THE GODLESS GIRL—Producers Distributing Corp.—from a story by Jeanie MacPherson.
CAST: Lina Basquette, George Duryea, Marie Prevost, Noah Beery, Mary Jane Irving, Gertrude Quality, Kate Price, Hedwig Reicher, Julia Faye, Emily Barrye, Jacqueline Dyrese.

1929: DYNAMITE—M.G.M.—from a story by Jeanie MacPherson.
CAST: Kay Johnson, Charles Bickford, Conrad Nagel, Julia Faye, Muriel McCormick.

1930: MADAM SATAN—M.G.M.—from a story by Edwin Milton Royle, Lucien Hubbard and Lenore Coffee—dialogue by Elsie Janis.
CAST: Kay Johnson, Reginald Denny, Roland Young, Elsie Peterson, Lillian Roth.

1931: THE SQUAW MAN—M.G.M.—from a play by Edwin Milton Royle—adapted by Jeanie MacPherson.
CAST: Warner Baxter, Eleanor Boardman, Paul Cavanaugh, Roland Young, Julia Faye, Lawrence Grant, Eva Dennison, Desmond Roberts, Lillian Bond, Harry Northrup, Lucille McIntosh, Lupe Velez, Mitchell Lewis, Charles Bickford, J. Farrell McDonald, Dickie Moore, De Witt Jennings, Raymond Hatton.

1932: THE SIGN OF THE CROSS—Paramount-Publix—from a play by Wilson Barrett—adapted by Waldemar Young and Sidney Buchman.
CAST: Frederic March, Elissa Landi, Charles Laughton, Claudette Colbert, Ian Keith, Genevieve Tobin, Ferdinand Gottschalk, Robert Manning.

1933: THIS DAY AND AGE—Paramount—from a story by Bartlett Cormack—adapted by Barlett Cormack and Lenore J. Coffee.
CAST: Charles Bickford, Judith Allen, Richard Cromwell, Harry Green, Eddie Nugent, Oscar Rudolph, Billy Gilbert.

1934: FOUR FRIGHTENED PEOPLE—Paramount—from a novel by E. Arnot Robertson—adapted by Bartlett Cormack and Lenore J. Coffee.
CAST: Claudette Colbert, Herbert Marshall, William Gargan, Mary Boland, Leo Carrillo.

1934: CLEOPATRA—Paramount—screenplay by Waldemar Young and Vincent Lawrence—adapted from historical material by Bartlett Cormack—contributors—Jeanie MacPherson and Finley Peter Dunne, Jr.
CAST: Claudette Colbert, Warren William, Henry Wilcoxon, Gertrude Michael, Joseph Schildkraut, Ian Keith, C. Aubrey Smith, William Farnum.

1935: THE CRUSADES—Paramount—screenplay by Harold Lamb, Waldemar Young, Dudley Nichols. Scenario by Jeanie MacPherson.
CAST: Loretta Young, Henry Wilcoxon, Ian Keith, C. Aubrey Smith, Katherine DeMille, Joseph Schildkraut, Alan Hale, C. Henry Gordon, George Barbier, Montagu Love, Lumsden Hare, William Farnum, Hobart Bosworth, Pedro de Cordoba, Mischa Auer, Jason Robards, J. Carrol Naish, Oscar Rudolph.

1937: THE PLAINSMAN—Paramount—screenplay by Waldemar Young, Harold Lamb and Lynn Riggs.
CAST: Gary Cooper, Jean Arthur, James Ellison, Charles Bickford, Helen Burgess.

1938: THE BUCCANEER—Paramount—based on "La Fitte the Pirate" by Lyle Saxon—screenplay by Edwin Justus Mayer, Harold Lamb and C. Gardiner Sullivan—adapted by Jeanie MacPherson.
CAST: Frederic March, Franciska Gaal, Akim Tamiroff, Margot Grahame, Walter Brennan, Ian Keith.

1939: UNION PACIFIC—Paramount—story by Ernest Haycox—adapted by Jack Cunningham—screenplay by Walter De Leon, C. Gardiner Sullivan and Jesse Lasky, Jr.
CAST: Barbara Stanwyck, Joel McCrea, Robert Preston, Lynn Overman, Akim Tamiroff, Brian Donlevy.

1940: NORTH WEST MOUNTED POLICE—Paramount—original screenplay by Allan LeMay, Jesse Lasky, Jr. and C. Gardiner Sullivan.
CAST: Gary Cooper, Madeleine Carroll, Paulette Goddard, Preston Foster, Robert Preston.

1942: REAP THE WILD WIND—Paramount—adapted from story by Thelma Strabel.
CAST: Ray Milland, John Wayne, Paulette Goddard, Raymond Massey, Robert Preston, Susan Hayward.

1944: THE STORY OF DR. WASSELL—Paramount—based on story related by 15 wounded World War II sailors to James Hilton.
CAST: Gary Cooper, Laraine Day, Signe Hasso, Dennis O'Keefe, Carol Thurston.

1947: UNCONQUERED—Paramount—from a novel by Neil H. Swanson.
CAST: Gary Cooper, Paulette Goddard, Howard da Silva, Boris Karloff, Cecil Kellaway, Ward Bond, Henry Wilcoxon, C. Aubrey Smith, Mike Mazzurki.

1949: SAMSON AND DELILAH—Paramount—original treatment by Harold Lamb and Vladimir Jobolinsky—also based on chapters 13–16 in Judges from the Bible.
CAST: Hedy La Marr, Victor Mature, George Sanders, Angela Lansbury, Henry Wilcoxon.

1952: THE GREATEST SHOW ON EARTH—Paramount—screenplay by Frederick M. Frank, Theodore St. John, and Frank Cavett.
CAST: Betty Hutton, Cornel Wilde, James Stewart, Charlton Heston, Dorothy Lamour, Gloria Grahame, Lyle Bettger, Henry Wilcoxon.

1956: THE TEN COMMANDMENTS—Paramount—Scenario by Jesse Lasky, Jr., Frederick M. Frank, Aeneas MacKenzie and Jack Gariss.
CAST: Charlton Heston, Yul Brynner, Anne Baxter, Edward G. Robinson, Yvonne De Carlo, Debra Paget, John Derek, Sir Cedric Hardwicke, Nina Foch, Martha Scott, Judith Anderson, Vincent Price, John Carradine, Olive Deering, Douglas Dumbrille, Frank De Kova, Henry Wilcoxon, Edward Franz, Donald Curtis, Lawrence Dobkin, H. B. Warner, Julia Faye.

Photo Fred H. Wright

About the Authors

Gabe Essoe is Director of Television Publicity at Walt Disney Studios and a freelance writer. In November 1967 his first book, *Gable,* also co-authored with Raymond Lee, was published. Since then he has written articles for such national magazines as *TV Guide, Yachting, Adam, Films in Review,* and major newspapers like the *Los Angeles Times, Chicago Daily News, Miami Herald;* and has had a second book, *Tarzan of the Movies,* published. He has just completed an in-depth volume, *The Films of Clark Gable,* and is currently writing his first novel and teleplay. His future plans include a book on the serials and concentration on screenplays. Besides writing, this talented new author paints in oils and enjoys refinishing furniture. His pretty young wife, Donna, is a dance instructor at Miraleste High School.

Raymond Lee has been one of filmland's leading historians for the past 20 years. A former child star, he has acted with most of the silent screen's greatest personalities. Retiring from movie life in 1936, he began writing plays, radio scripts, short stories, and articles. After a hitch in the Air Corps during World War II, he returned to Hollywood and became the editor of *Offbeat Magazine,* and also wrote a column. His books include *Fit for the Chase* (a story of movie cars) and *Not So Dumb* (which discusses filmland's animal stars). He is the co-author, with Clarence Bull, of *Faces of Hollywood* (a gallery of portraits of Hollywood's leading film personalities). With Manuel Weltman he has written *Pearl White, the Peerless Fearless Girl.* In the works are a book on Gloria Swanson and another on movie cowboys.